DESIGNING TESSELLATIONS

The Secrets
of Interlocking
Patterns

DESIGNING

CB
CONTEMPORARY BOOKS

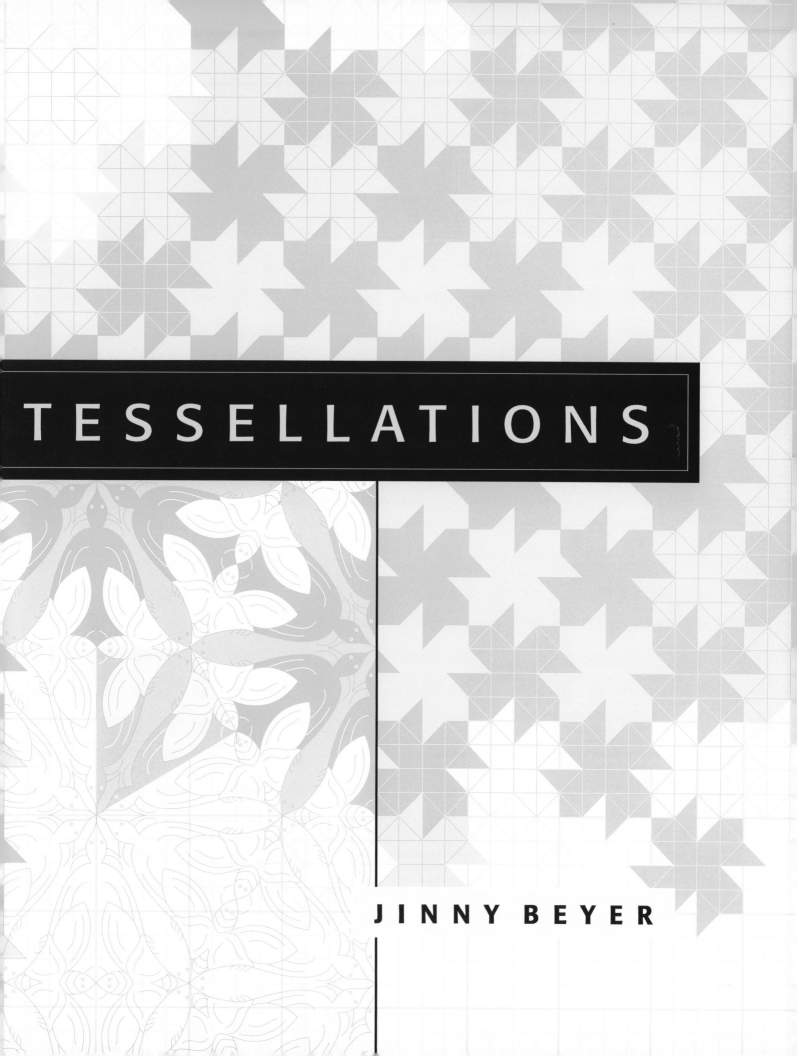

TESSELLATIONS

JINNY BEYER

Library of Congress Cataloging-in-Publication Data

Beyer, Jinny.
    Designing tessellations : the secrets of interlocking patterns / Jinny Beyer.
       p.   cm.
    Includes bibliographical references.
    ISBN 0-8092-2866-1
    1. Quilting.   2. Patchwork.   3. Quilts—Design.   4. Patchwork quilts—
Design.   I. Title.
TT835.B429   1998
746.46′041—dc21   98-13128
                                            CIP

Editorial and production direction by Anne Knudsen
Art direction and interior design by Kim Bartko
Cover design by Monica Baziuk
Interior layouts by Mary C. Lockwood
Production editing by Michelle Davidson
Technical drawings by Kandy Petersen
Manufacturing direction by Pat Martin
Quilt photography by Steve Tuttle, unless specifically credited
Picture research by Elizabeth Broadrup Lieberman

Published by Contemporary Books
A division of NTC/Contemporary Publishing Group, Inc.
4255 West Touhy Avenue, Lincolnwood (Chicago), Illinois 60646-1975 U.S.A.
Copyright © 1999 by Jinny Beyer
Printed in Singapore
International Standard Book Number: 0-8092-2866-1
99 00 01 02 03 04 SS 20 19 18 17 16 15 14 13 12 11 10 9 8 7 6 5 4 3 2 1

To the memory of M. C. Escher. His genius for creating intricate interlocking patterns has delighted artists and artisans for decades. His work inspired me on the quest for discovery and experimentation that resulted in Designing Tessellations.

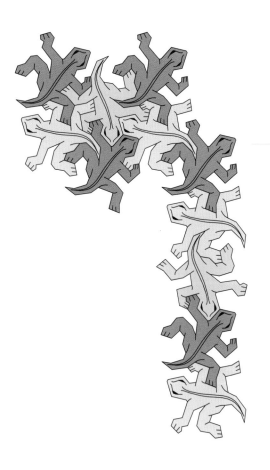

Contents

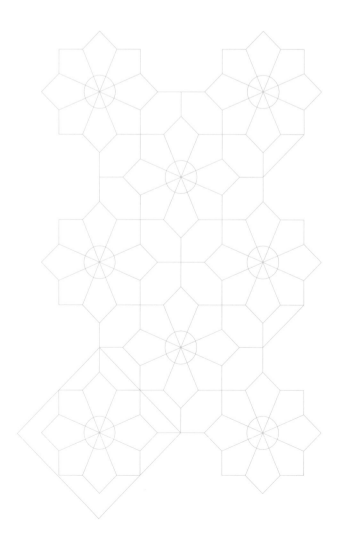

American Woven Coverlet

Introduction

Geometric design has been an integral part of my life for the last 25 years. During that time I have often wondered why it was that I almost flunked high school geometry. The class was drudgery and so very difficult that I gave up taking further math courses. Yet as an adult, when I first became interested in surface design, it was geometric patterns that intrigued me more than any others.

Shortly after we were married, my husband and I lived for several years in various countries in the Orient. I was intrigued by the incredibly beautiful geometric designs that adorned the walls, floors, and windows of the palaces, temples, mosques, and shrines we visited. The structure and the repeat of those patterns across a surface fascinated me. I wanted to know how those designs were created and to be able to reproduce them myself.

My interest in design has followed many courses, but it was shortly after our return from the Orient in the early 1970s that I began exploring the world of geometric patterns in earnest, and that was in the field of quilt making. The block motifs of the quilts themselves inspired me, but I was equally excited by seeing how those patterns changed as various symmetrical arrangements were applied to them. My love of geometric patterns continued as my career progressed into textile design. It is a constant challenge to figure out how various designs are made and how to make new ones. I also get immense enjoyment from showing others how easy it is to design, create, and draft geometric designs for use in any area of surface design.

That high school geometry class was difficult because it was no fun. All we did was memorize formulas and do equations. Much later, I learned with excitement the versatility of geometric motifs in pattern design. I was sorry that my teacher had not applied the geometric lessons to more concrete examples and that my mind had not been ready to absorb the information.

Tessellations

One of the first tessellated designs I saw more than 20 years ago was the popular quilt pattern known as *Spool* or *Indian Hatchet*. Without knowing it was a tessellation, the design appealed to me immediately. I set about to recreate it. My attempts at first frustrated me. Then, with delight, I noticed how the curves in the pattern fit together, one into the next, flowing smoothly across the surface. I was hooked.

When I found a book on M. C. Escher's work I was enthralled yet mystified. His graphic designs relied on incredibly complicated interlocking patterns and designs. Sometimes more than one image joined with another. It was beyond me how those patterns were created, and the books written on the subject reminded me of that high school geometry class; the terminology and explanations were over my head.

I knew one day I would take the time to study and try to figure it all out. That time came almost six years ago. Working on it ever since, I have made the most incredible journey; a journey that has flung open a door to new design opportunities; a journey that has led to an understanding of symmetry in nature and surface design; and a journey that has given

Modified Spool, antique charm quilt, quilter unknown, c. 1880.

me the key to unlock the mysteries of Escher's art that had seemed so out of reach. Once the lightbulbs started going on, it became so simple. In *Designing Tessellations*, I want to share my experiences and discoveries, and make it easier for others to work with tessellating designs.

Symmetry and Tessellations Intertwined

Tessellations and symmetry go hand in hand. A knowledge of symmetrical design is essential for full comprehension of tessellations. And, once an understanding of tessellations has been achieved, the numerous applications of symmetry to tessellated designs makes them even more exciting.

Kashmir Shawl

Escher studied the theory of tessellating designs extensively. He developed his own classification system for creating and defining tessellating motifs. Crystallographers and mathematicians have explained the theories in mathematical terms, but to the layperson who does not have advanced mathematical degrees the terminology and explanations can seem daunting.

As I studied Escher and experimented with tessellating motifs, I worked out the system that seemed to make the most sense to *me*. I present my own system here, in hopes that I will not offend the mathematicians, but with a desire to share my knowledge with others who, like me, want to understand the basics of creating tessellating design, but who may not have studied math. This book is for you, so you do not have to struggle as I did or wade through formulas or give up in frustration. It is not enough for me just to tell you what to do; it is important for you

Birds and Fish
by Jinny Beyer.

to understand what you are doing and what you hope to achieve. Once that understanding takes place, there is freedom for experimentation and creativity that is uniquely rewarding.

Because of the interrelationship between symmetry and tessellations this book will first explore the wonders of linear and two-dimensional symmetry and will then lead you into the exciting world of tessellations. With a few simple guidelines the design possibilities are endless, whether you wish to create geometric designs that interlock perfectly over a surface or whether you are making representational tessellations in the style of M. C. Escher. No matter what element of surface design you are interested in—quilts, stained glass, fabric design, graphics, and more—experiment, work through the book from the beginning, and create tessellated motifs to use in whatever medium you choose.

Acknowledgments

For almost 20 years I have conducted an annual quilting seminar on Hilton Head Island in South Carolina. Working with a talented group of quilters, together we plan each year's seminar theme, always endeavoring to develop new ideas and new ways to teach concepts to participants. The seminars in 1993, 1996, and 1997 dealt with mosaic design, tessellations, and symmetry, respectively, all subjects that helped to form the content of this book.

I would like to thank the members of the seminar staff who worked with me during those years: Luella Bauer, Danielle Brower-Naber, Laura Chapman, Darlene Christopherson, JoAnn Dawson, Helen Fairchild, Patricia Germann, Paula Golden, Jennifer Heffernan, Nancy Johnson, Brenda Jones, Bunnie Jordan, Kathryn Kuhn, Kay Lettau, Patti Marcus, Jay Moody, Robin Morrison, Carole Nicholas, Lenore Parham, Andrea Perkins, Linda Pool, Kaye Rhodes, Gayle Ropp, Yoko Sawanobori, Judy Spahn, Ellen Swanson, Barbara Tricarico, and Terri Willett. Without the aid of the seminar staff, the book could not have materialized. Not only did their input help in developing the concepts presented here, but many of their quilts are also shown in the book.

Thanks also go to Barbara Dean for allowing her quilt to appear, to Kay and David McClain and to Mary Alice and Richard Malesarti for the use of quilts from their collections (*Chorus Line Choreography* and *Yellow Houses*, respectively). Thank you to Steven Tuttle for his expert photography, to mathematicians Kevin Lee and Doris Schattschneider for their advice, to Kandy Petersen for illustrations, to Dan Ramsey, illustration consultant, and to my editor Anne Knudsen, art director Kim Bartko, graphic designer Mary Lockwood, project editor Michelle Davidson, image specialists Todd Petersen and Michael Brown, picture researcher Elizabeth Broadrup Lieberman, and all the staff at Contemporary Books.

And finally thank you to my husband, John, for his love and support during the creation of this project.

Day Lilies, *Jinny Beyer*, 1998.
This quilt is an example of six rotation (p6) symmetry. The tessellating design was developed from a 60° diamond. See page 177 for details.

CHAPTER 1

What Are *Tessellations*?

THE FIRST QUESTION that most people ask when I talk about my work is "What is a *tessellation*?" The word sounds so mysterious. Actually, tessellations are easy to understand. We are exposed to them on a daily basis. A tessellation is simply a shape or tile that repeats to fill a surface without any gaps or overlaps. The diagrams on the next page illustrate this. A tile can be repeated in a linear row for a one-dimensional design, or it can be repeated both vertically and horizontally for a two-dimensional pattern. The name comes from the word *tessella*, the small square tile used in ancient Roman mosaics.

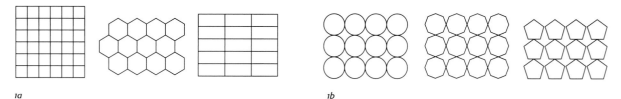

1a   1b

Illustration 1.1. The shapes in Illustration 1.1a are tiles because they fill the surface without any gaps. The shapes in Illustration 1.1b are not tiles because they do not join together without gaps.

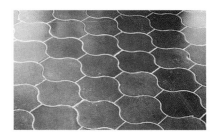

Floor tile from Las Palmas Hotel, Los Barriles, Mexico.

Detail of Akbar's tomb in Sikandra, India. This structure contains a vast array of interlocking patterns.

The diagrams above illustrate some simple tiles and other familiar shapes that are not tiles because they do not fill the surface without gaps.

From Simple Tessellations to Escher-Type Designs

We are exposed to tile or tessellated patterns every day—bathroom or floor tiles, brick paths, patterns on fabrics, wallpapers, and so much more. Today, however, the types of designs that most people associate with tessellations are the interlocking patterns of the type for which artist M. C. Escher is famous. His genius has intrigued artists and designers for decades.

Some Escher tessellations are shown opposite. When I first saw Escher's work I was overwhelmed. How could anyone figure out a design where the head of a bird would nestle into the legs and belly of another identical bird; where birds and fish are intertwined; or where identical interlocking fish alternate rows, swimming one direction, then another? I also became more and more intrigued with the interlocking tile patterns found in so many ancient designs, many of which have been used for centuries in various types of surface designs including mosaic walls, floors, windows, and textiles like the ones shown on this page.

In essence, all of these tessellating motifs are simply tiles, tiles that continually repeat to form a pattern without any gaps or overlaps. The key to the mystery is in recognizing how the tile is created.

Symmetry Drawing E128 *by M. C. Escher.*

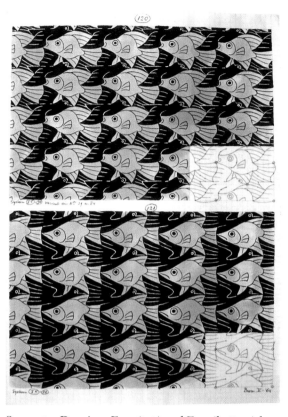

Symmetry Drawings E120 *(top) and* E121 *(bottom) by M. C. Escher.*

Symmetry Drawing E24 *by M. C. Escher.*

Symmetry Drawing E25 *(Reptiles) by M. C. Escher.*

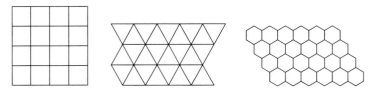

Illustration 1.2. *Squares, triangles, and hexagons are tiles, or tessellations, as they fit together without any gaps or overlaps.*

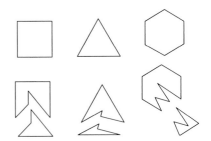

Illustration 1.3. **When a piece is taken away from a square, triangle, or hexagon, it is no longer a tile, since multiples of these will not fit together without gaps or overlaps.**

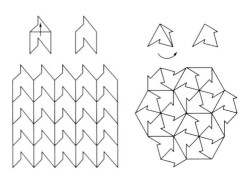

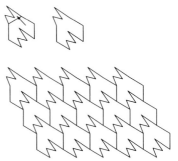

Illustration 1.4. **If the piece that was taken away is given back to another side of the shape, a tile is created, as multiples of those shapes will once again fit together without any gaps or overlaps.**

If you begin with very basic shapes, the making of a tessellation becomes apparent. A square is a very simple tile, or tessellation. Multiple squares can fit together indefinitely without any gaps or overlaps. A hexagon is a tessellation. Multiple hexagons can also fit together side by side to fill a surface without any gaps or overlaps, and the same holds true for equilateral triangles and many other shapes. (See Illustration 1.2.)

As soon as you take a chunk or piece away from the square, hexagon, or triangle, you no longer have a tessellation; the pieces can no longer fit together without any gaps or overlaps. (See Illustration 1.3.)

If the piece is taken away you no longer have a tessellation, but if it is given back to the shape you will once again have the tessellation. That is the key to understanding interlocking tessellated designs. The piece that was taken away can be put back into the same hole to reform the shape, or it can be put back onto one of the other sides of the shape. Illustration 1.4 shows what happens when the pieces that were taken from the square, hexagon, and triangle are given back to another side of the shape. A new tile has been created that will fit together over and over without any gaps or overlaps.

There are many ways a piece that has been taken away can be given back. It can be moved to an opposite side or to an adjacent side. It can be flipped before being given back. It can be given back and then the tile can be mirrored, flipped, or rotated.

Illustration 1.5 shows the same square with the same chunk cut from it as in Illustration 1.3, but now the chunk has been given back in a variety of ways.

When you see how different the square can look with only one piece cut from a single side, imagine the multitude of possibilities if you then go back and cut a piece from one of the other unaltered sides. The number of ways to create tessellated

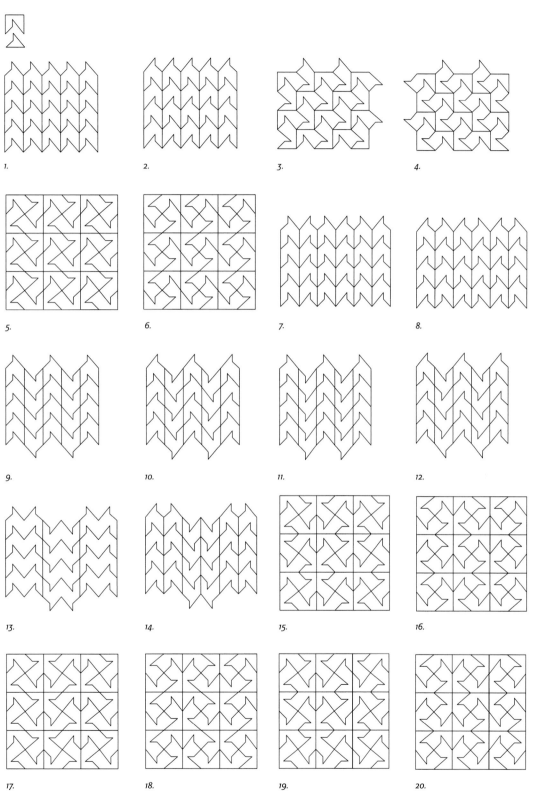

Illustration 1.5. These illustrations show the patterns created by taking the identical piece from a square, giving it back, and arranging the resulting shape in a variety of ways.

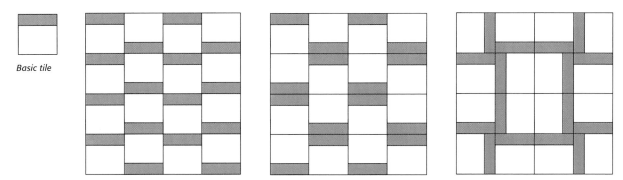

Basic tile

Illustration 1.6. Some of the design possibilities for layout of the basic tile are shown on these two pages.

patterns and the ways in which those patterns can be laid out leads us to the study of symmetry, an understanding of which will allow for a full exploration of tessellating designs.

Symmetry and Tessellations

Many tiles have designs inside their own boundaries, and even though what occurs inside the tile does not affect how adjacent tiles fit together, that design can dramatically alter the appearance of the pattern that is created when tiles are put together. For instance, many square bathroom tiles have patterns across one of the edges, some even as simple as a line. Those tiles can all be oriented in the same way and put together over and over to fill a surface, or they can be turned in various ways and then put together, as shown in the examples above (Illustration 1.6). It is the way in which tiles are put together and the symmetries that each placement creates that lead to the overall designs.

Symmetry is a system for organizing repeating parts of a design. In surface design there are 17 ways in which repeating parts can be arranged to fill a surface (two-dimensional design). There are seven ways in which the parts can be arranged to create a linear pattern (one-dimensional design). When added together these 24 ways are the basis for all surface ornamental patterns, including wallpaper, textiles, quilts, and graphic design.

Symmetry and tessellations are inevitably intertwined and an understanding of one leads to a better comprehension of the

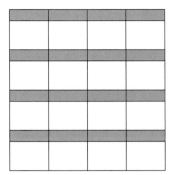 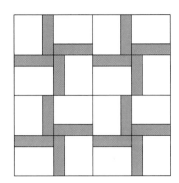 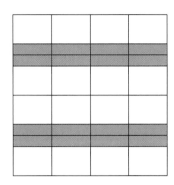

other. Chapters 2 through 5 explain in detail the principles of one- and two-dimensional symmetry. They are presented with exercises that allow you to experiment with symmetry. Working with paper, scissors, and tape, you will move shapes around in different ways, seeing exactly how they fit together to create symmetrical patterns. You will learn more easily and quickly if you do each exercise, as they help clarify concepts and give you immediate results. You will see as you work how exciting the principles of symmetry can be especially once you are able to apply them to your own artistic medium.

Whatever your design interest, these simple exercises will allow you to discover a multitude of ways that a single motif can change simply by the way in which it is moved about a surface.

Chapters 7 through 11 will take you step-by-step through the processes for creating interlocking tiles and patterns. We explore both geometric designs that are popular in such media as mosaic work, wallpaper design, and textiles and quilt making and the more representational images for which M. C. Escher is celebrated. It is important for you to have an understanding of symmetry before going on to these chapters, as it will make understanding the principles of creating tessellating designs so much easier. You will also have the knowledge to create even more designs by applying the various symmetries to the tessellations you create.

Take your time to read carefully, study the illustrations, work through the exercises, and most of all enjoy applying everything you learn to enrich your own designs.

Castle Keep, *Jinny Beyer, 1981.*
This quilt is an example of traditional block (p4m) symmetry.
See page 12 to find out how the pattern is formed.

CHAPTER 2

An Introduction to *Symmetry*

PATTERN AND SYMMETRY are as old as rhythm and communication and are found in every culture, no matter how primitive. Symmetry surrounds us, both in terms of what occurs naturally in our environment and in what has been created by the human mind and hand. It is symmetry that creates a pattern. It is a basic organizing principle, a system of repeating parts that forms a design. Symmetry begins when a nonsymmetrical motif (a *cell*) is repeated to form a pattern. How that motif is repeated determines how the pattern will look, and one single cell can be repeated in a wide variety of ways to produce many different designs. A clear understanding of symmetry is essential to creating tessellating patterns.

Pattern

A pattern is an organization or arrangement of repeating parts. Within nature, art, and music, a pattern relies on three characteristics: a single part or cell, a repetition of that part, and a system of organizing those repeating parts. A study of the photographs on this page will show that in each one there is a part or cell that repeats to form some type of pattern. Any time a cell or part is repeated more than once, there will be a pattern.

The natural world is full of wondrous patterns and designs. While going for a walk, you might discern pattern in the leaves, trees, flowers, and rocks. Animals will naturally form a pattern—birds flying in formation, fish swimming in a school, or herds protecting themselves. Some inbred instinct causes them to behave in a symmetrical way. The wings of a butterfly form a pattern, as one wing is the mirror image of the other; a snowflake forms a beautiful pattern as crystals repeat; and leaves on a branch grow in a repetitive design.

Pattern and ornament are as old as creation, and the reproducing of patterns has been a basic design principle throughout the history of humankind, often inspired by the beautiful patterns found in nature. Look around your home. There is pattern in an Oriental carpet, a piece of fabric, wallpaper, the arrangement of keys on a keyboard, the panes of glass in a window. Study of architecture, both historic and modern, reveals repetitive parts forming patterns that please the eye.

Patterns in fabric are usually made up of repeating elements. In fact many fabrics are designed so that the repeating elements fit together to create an overall pattern. As illustrated in the fabrics shown here, it is very difficult to see where the tiles fit together. The repeating elements of a motif can be arranged in different ways to form a variety of different patterns. Each way a motif is repeated to form a pattern is a type of symmetry.

Illustration 2.1. Examples of patterns found in fabric.

School House block primary cell

Illustration 2.2. Yellow Houses, made by Judy Spahn in 1983, is a variation of the traditional School House design. The single unit, or primary cell, used to create the pattern has been isolated at the left.

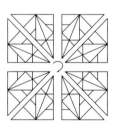

This small unit repeats to form the pattern.

Four mirrored pairs of the small unit rotate to form the block.

Completed Castle Keep block. This block repeats over and over to form the pattern of the quilt.

Illustration 2.3. The smaller unit that repeats to form the design of Castle Keep is shown here along with four mirrored pairs of the unit that form the repeating tile.

Illustration 2.4. Detail from Castle Keep, a traditional block quilt (see page 8).

Illustration 2.5. Detail of Water Lily *(see page 180). There is linear symmetry in the patchwork border as well as the fabric border.*

During the last 25 years with the resurgence of interest in handcrafts, thousands of people have experimented with surface design in weaving, various textile arts, and quilt making.

Analyzing traditional quilt patterns is an excellent approach to the study of symmetry, as most are made up of multiples of single units that are repeated to create the design. In the traditional *School House* quilt block, the block itself is the single unit or cell that repeats to form the design. In *Castle Keep*, shown on page 8 and in Illustration 2.4, multiple smaller units first form the design of the block and then the block is repeated across the surface of the quilt.

Illustration 2.6. Several examples of one-dimensional symmetry can be seen in this architectural detail from the Taj Mahal in Agra, India.

Types of Symmetry

Symmetry is a basic organizing principle; it is a system of arranging repeating parts to form a pattern. There are various types of patterns that can be created with symmetrical movements. A daffodil, daisy, chandelier, or football all have symmetry, but in surface design, which is what this book is about, there are two types of symmetrical patterns to study. One of those is motions that create one-dimensional linear or *frieze* symmetrical patterns, in which the repeating parts go only in one direction, as shown in Illustrations 2.5 and 2.6.

The other type of pattern created with symmetrical motions is two-dimensional or *wallpaper* designs, in which the repeating parts go in both directions filling an entire surface such as tiles on a floor, a mosaic mural, or blocks in a quilt. Look at the example in Illustration 2.7.

Illustration 2.7. Two-dimensional symmetry, in a detail from the Taj Mahal.

Patterns in Fabric and Wallpaper

Hand block-printing on fabric. The fabric is hanging to dry. Circa 1800.

For centuries prior to the invention of modern printing devices, patterns for fabrics were carved out of wood and the repeat of the pattern was carefully engineered. The fabric was laboriously printed by dipping the woodblock into dye and then carefully stamping it onto the cloth until the entire surface was covered with the design. One block was used for each color in the design. Woodblock printing was introduced to the Europeans in the 1600s by way of their calico trade with India, and the technique was used for printing both fabric and wallpaper.

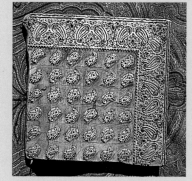

Scottish woodblock embedded with metal used for hand block-printing of fabric.

In the mid-1700s copper-plate printing was first used on cloth. A design was engraved on a large sheet of copper, which was as wide as the cloth and one yard long. In this method a larger surface could be printed at one time, thus speeding up the process immeasurably. Since the tile (translation unit) was larger, there could be more design elements before it had to repeat. The limitation was that only one color could be printed, so woodblock printing continued to be used for multicolored patterns.

In the early 1800s the fabric industry was revolutionized with the invention of the roller printing machine. In this technique the pattern was engraved on cylindrical copper rollers and the cloth could be printed continuously, with a different roller for each color. The repeat of the tile was the circumference of the rollers, which were mounted on huge machines.

Hand-printing of fabric from woodblock. Sanganar, India.

An article in an 1852 *Godey's Lady's Book* said of roller printing: "The invention of roller-printing is the greatest achievement that has been made in the art. A length of calico equal to one mile can, by this method, be printed off with four different colors in one hour, and more accurately and with better effect than block printing by hand. . . . one cylinder machine, attended by one man, can perform as much work in the same time as one hundred men attended by one hundred children."

Technology remained virtually the same for more than 150 years, until the screen-printing process began to be used. Patterns changed because the delicate designs achieved with engraved rollers could not be duplicated on screens. Gradually screen-printing techniques have improved, making printing faster and more efficient. As a result, roller printing machines are being phased out.

When I began designing fabrics in 1981, the plant that printed my designs had 12 roller machines. Those old machines, some of which were originals from the 1800s, were gradually retired (actually put in the field behind the plant to rust), and in June of 1995 the last machine was removed. By the early part of the twenty-first century there will probably be no roller printing done on fabric anywhere in the world.

Throughout all of the processes of printing fabric or wallpaper during the past centuries, the design concepts have remained the same. Begin with an individual cell or part and then repeat that part in various ways to create a tile (translation unit), such as a woodblock, a copper plate, or a copper roller, and repeat that tile over and over to achieve a pattern.

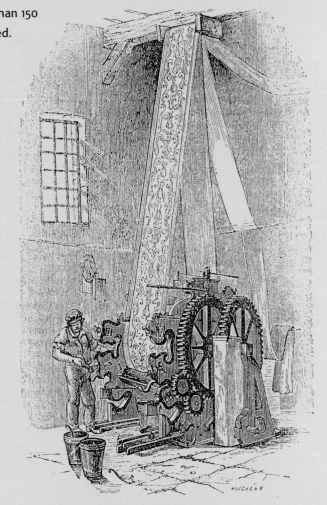

Roller printing machine.

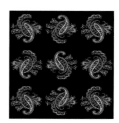

Illustration 2.8. Four different repetitions of a paisley motif, with primary cell isolated.

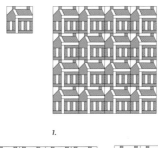

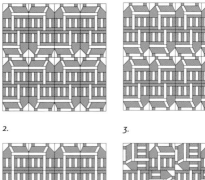

1.

2.   3.

4.   5.

Illustration 2.9. Five variations on the School House *quilt block, with primary cell isolated.*

There are only a few fundamental principles to learn concerning one- and two-dimensional symmetrical patterns, and these are the basis of all pattern organization and design. Once you gain an understanding of how a pattern is made, you will be able to apply that to the creation of your own patterns.

The pattern of a design can look very different even when the same initial block or cell is used, depending on how those blocks are arranged. Fabrics created from a single paisley motif can look quite different depending on how that paisley motif has been repeated, as shown in the examples in Illustration 2.8. The examples in Illustration 2.9 show the popular quilt design *School House* and a few of the many patterns that can be formed by placing the blocks in various ways.

Asymmetry is the absence of symmetry, yet an asymmetrical motif is essential for the formation of a symmetrical pattern. The paisley motif used in the fabric design is asymmetrical, it has no repeating parts, but as soon as that paisley is repeated in different ways, it forms a symmetrical pattern as shown in Illustration 2.8. The *School House* design is asymmetrical. It has no

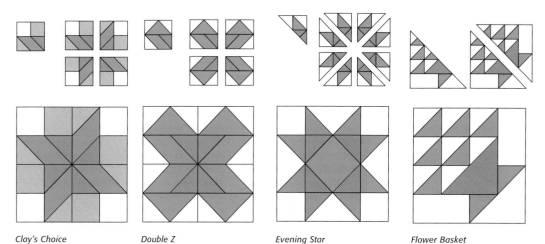

Clay's Choice   Double Z   Evening Star   Flower Basket

Illustration 2.10. Traditional quilt blocks with primary cell isolated.

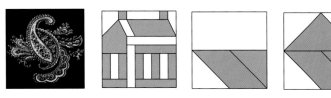

Illustration 2.11. Primary cells.

Illustration 2.12. Primary cells forming a
linear pattern.

repeating parts, but as it is repeated in different ways, it forms various symmetrical patterns as can be seen in Illustration 2.9.

Four traditional quilt designs are shown in Illustration 2.10. In each case the asymmetrical unit that forms the design is isolated so you can see how that motif repeats to form the pattern.

Primary Cell

The asymmetrical motif, which repeats to form a pattern, has been called various names in the discussion of symmetry (primitive cell, generating unit, unit cell, etc.). In this book it will be referred to as the *primary cell* or simply *cell*. For our purposes, the primary cell always contains an asymmetric motif. It is the smallest portion of the pattern that repeats. Once you can look at a pattern and learn how to break it down to find its primary cell, a wealth of design possibilities will open up to you. The motifs in Illustration 2.11 are all primary cells: the paisley unit that forms a fabric design, the *School House* quilt block, and the portions of two other quilt designs, *Clay's Choice* and *Double Z*.

Tile

I use the word *tile* to describe the unit that is repeated over and over to create the pattern. Mathematicians have called this a *translation unit*. The tiles or translation units will always be oriented in the same direction. They must fit together without any gaps or overlaps, and they must completely fill the surface. The primary cell in itself can be the tile. For instance in one-dimensional symmetry the primary cell could repeat side by side to form a linear pattern as shown in Illustration 2.12. Or the primary cell can repeat in both directions to fill the surface, as in Illustration 2.13. The tile can also be a group of two or more primary cells arranged in some fashion to form the tile. Each of the primary cells shown in Illustration 2.14 has once again been arranged in

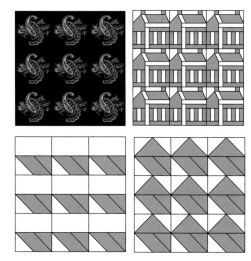

Illustration 2.13. Primary cells forming a two-
dimensional pattern.

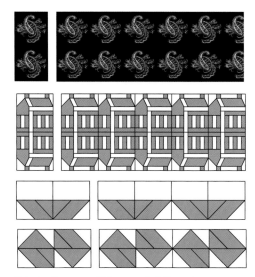

Illustration 2.14. Tiles created from two
cells to create a linear pattern.

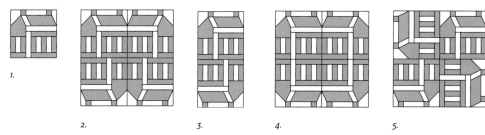

1.

2.   *3.*   *4.*   *5.*

Illustration 2.15. These tiles form the patterns shown on page 16.

Illustration 2.16. Pattern formed from quilt block tiles shown in Illustration 2.10.

a linear, one-directional fashion, but now the tile is a combination of two or more cells rather than the primary cell alone. (See illustration 2.14.)

Look again at the illustrations of the *School House* blocks and the paisley fabrics on page 16. In each one of those a group of primary cells has been put together to form a tile and then that tile repeats to form the pattern. The individual tiles used to create the *School House* illustration are shown in Illustration 2.15, and the numbers reference the illustrations that they match.

In Illustration 2.10 you saw how four traditional quilt blocks were broken down into their primary cells. The quilt blocks are the tiles, which are made up of a combination of those cells. Those blocks or tiles, repeated in two directions, fill the surface and create a type of pattern popular in many quilts. (See Illustration 2.16.)

The basis of symmetrical surface design is to have a tile (translation unit) that orients in the same direction and repeats with no gaps or overlaps. Therefore, only certain shapes can be used as tiles. Circles, most pentagons, octagons, and many other

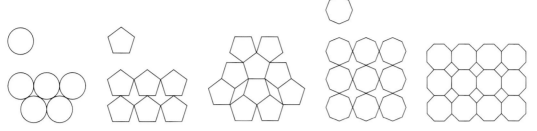

Illustration 2.17. These shapes cannot be tiles because they do not fit together without gaps.

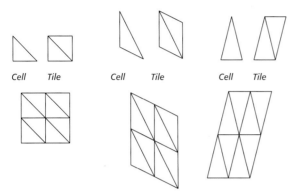

Illustration 2.18. It takes two triangles to form a tile.

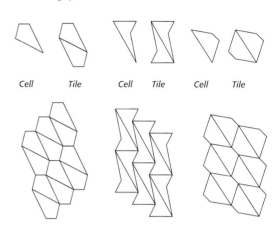

Illustration 2.19. All quadrilaterals fit together without gaps, but if opposite sides are not parallel and equal in length, it takes two of each to form a tile.

multisided shapes are not tiles because gaps are created when they are put side by side. (See Illustration 2.17.)

All triangles will join together without gaps or overlaps, but to fit correctly, one has to be turned upside down or flipped. Therefore the tile is not the triangle by itself, but a combination of two triangles, which then form a four-sided shape, as in Illustration 2.18.

All four-sided shapes (quadrilaterals) will fit together without gaps or overlaps; however, if opposite sides are not equal in length or parallel to each other, one will have to be turned upside down to the other for them to fit together to form a tile, as in Illustration 2.19. Hexagons will also work as long as opposite sides are parallel and equal in length.

Tiles used for symmetrical designs, therefore, are limited to quadrilaterals (four-sided shapes) and hexagons (six-sided shapes). However in order for those tiles to be oriented in the same direction, opposite sides of the shapes must be parallel to each other and equal in length. Other shapes can be contained within the tile, but when the cells form the final tile, that tile must be in the form of a quadrilateral or a hexagon, with opposite sides parallel and equal, as in Illustration 2.20.

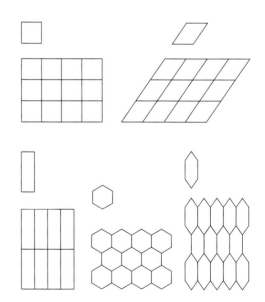

Illustration 2.20. Tiles or translation units are single or multiple cells that form hexagons or quadrilaterals with opposite sides that are parallel and equal in length.

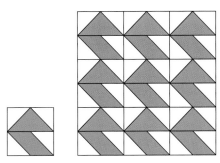

Illustration 2.21. Translation.

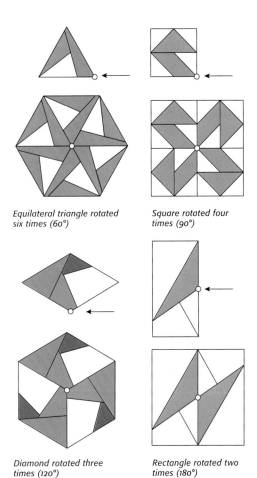

Equilateral triangle rotated six times (60°)

Square rotated four times (90°)

Diamond rotated three times (120°)

Rectangle rotated two times (180°)

Illustration 2.22. Examples of rotation.

Ways to Generate Symmetrical Patterns

There are four motions that generate all linear and two-dimensional symmetries. These four motions are easy to remember, and a knowledge of them will help you in designing all symmetrical and tessellated designs.

Translation

The first method of generating a pattern is called *translation*. In translation the primary cell is the tile. It is always oriented in the same direction and is moved sideways, vertically, or diagonally, as shown in Illustration 2.21.

Rotation

The second method of manipulating a cell is by *rotation*. In rotation the primary cell is rotated a certain number of times. The number of rotations depends on the shape of the primary cell and the angle around which the rotation takes place. In rotation the cell is not flipped but merely turned. In the examples in Illustration 2.22, the equilateral triangle has been rotated six times to create the hexagonal tile. The square has been rotated four times to create a square tile, the diamond has been rotated three times to create a hexagonal tile, and the rectangle has been rotated two times to create a square tile. In all cases the arrow indicates the place where the rotation occurred.

Mirror

The third method of generating a pattern from a primary cell is through *mirroring*. This is also called "reflecting." In mirroring, one or more sides of the primary cell are reflected. When generating patterns that have mirrors, you need to create two ver-

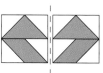
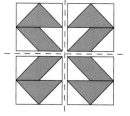
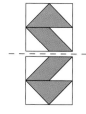

Vertical mirror   Horizontal mirror   Vertical and horizontal mirror
                                                    (double mirror)

Illustration 2.23. Mirror.

sions of the primary cell, one that is the mirror image of the other. Imagine that you have two cells on pieces of clear acetate. Stack them on top of each other oriented in exactly the same way and open the top one just as you would open a book. Imagine there is a hinge on the side. In essence you are moving the cell and then flipping it. If the cell is moved horizontally it is flipped horizontally. (This is referred to as a vertical mirror because the mirror line runs in a vertical direction.) If it is moved vertically it is flipped vertically. (Because the mirror line runs in a horizontal direction this is referred to as a horizontal mirror.) The examples in Illustration 2.23 show a primary cell that has been mirrored on one side, on the bottom, and on both the sides and the bottom. The dotted lines indicate where the cell has been mirrored.

Glide

The fourth way to generate a pattern from a primary cell is by a *glide*. A glide is a combination of a translation and a mirror (reflection), thus it is usually referred to as a glide reflection, but I find it easier to call it simply a glide. There are three types of glides, horizontal, vertical and diagonal. These operations can be achieved in various ways, but this is what works best for me. For a horizontal glide the cell is moved horizontally and flipped vertically (2.24a). With a vertical glide the cell is moved vertically and flipped horizontally (2.24b). This is in contrast to the mirror in which the cell is flipped the same direction as it is moved. In a diagonal glide the flip (or reflection) occurs on one of the corners of the cell and then the cell is moved so that its side abuts to either of the two sides of the original cell that is adjacent to the reflected corner (2.24c). In this text, because of space constraints and the pertinence to interlocking patterns, we only explore patterns based on horizontal or vertical glides, but the reader should be aware that in symmetry groups that are based

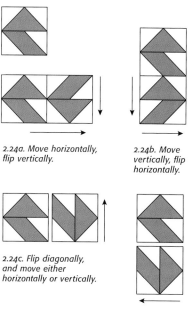

2.24a. Move horizontally, flip vertically.

2.24b. Move vertically, flip horizontally.

2.24c. Flip diagonally, and move either horizontally or vertically.

Illustration 2.24. Glide.

1.

2.

3.

4.

5.

6.

7.

8.

9.

10.

11.

12.

13.

14.

15.

16.

17.

Illustration 2.25. Patterns representing each of the 17 two-dimensional symmetry groups.

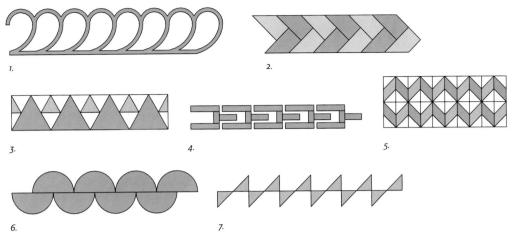

Illustration 2.26. Patterns representing each of the seven linear symmetry groups.

on glide reflections, additional patterns can be achieved with diagonal glides of the primary cell.

These four operations—translation, rotation, mirror, and glide—and combinations of them will generate 7 linear or border symmetries (also known as frieze symmetries) and 17 two-dimensional symmetries (often called wallpaper symmetries).

Illustrations 2.25 and 2.26 show examples of designs that have been created with the 17 two-dimensional and 7 linear symmetries. It may seem a complete puzzle as to how some of the patterns were created, but the solution is very simple. If you read through this book systematically, do the exercises, and study the examples, before long you will be able to look at any design, find the primary cell, and understand how that design was generated. More important, you will be able to create your own designs using the various symmetry operations. Appendixes A and B tell what each of these symmetries is. After you have read the next three chapters, come back to this page and see if you can figure out the symmetry of the designs before checking in the appendix.

Chapter 3 explains in detail the first 11 two-dimensional symmetry groups, which can all be generated from a square primary cell. Chapter 4 covers the remaining six symmetry groups, which have shapes other than a square as the primary cell. Chapter 5 explains the seven one-dimensional border or frieze symmetry groups. Once you understand how to work with movements of an unaltered shape that create patterns in these symmetry groups, it will be much clearer how to alter the shapes and use the same symmetry operations to create interlocking or tessellating patterns.

The Two-Dimensional Symmetry Labels

Labeling or naming the 17 two-dimensional symmetry groups has been achieved in many different ways by different writers and mathematicians. The following information is given because when you begin studying symmetry you may want to know why the symmetry groups are labeled the way they are. Don't try to understand the labeling system fully at this point. Skim over this part, go on to the next two chapters, then come back and read this section again. It will make a lot more sense after you have read in detail about each of the symmetry groups and how it is produced.

When I first began studying symmetry I found the labeling systems confusing, and it was much easier for me to attach my own labels to the groups. My own labels seemed the most logical to me in terms of exactly how I was manipulating the cells, and they seem to make symmetry less confusing for the students I teach. However, as I became more familiar with the symmetry groups, the standard labels began to make more sense and I now use both interchangeably. This book will use the label I have attached to each symmetry group with the shortened standard label listed next to it in parentheses.

The notation system for naming the 17 two-dimensional symmetry groups that has become standard is explained in an article written by Doris Schattschneider for the *American Mathematical Monthly*, 85, 1978, titled, "The Plane Symmetry Groups: Their Recognition and Notation."

The system is the two-dimensional counterpart of that used by crystallographers to classify crystals, and for this reason the 17 wallpaper symmetries are sometimes called two-dimensional crystallographic groups. The crystallographic notation looks at the pattern as a whole and not necessarily at the individual parts. As a designer, I am more interested in how the individual parts create the pattern. In many instances there is more than one way to create the same pattern, thus sometimes causing confusion among designers as to the crystallographer's notation. My goal here is to explain the notation system as it makes the most sense to me and, in so doing, to make it clear to other people who are interested in creating patterns. My apologies to the crystallographers for any liberties I may have taken with their labels. I am particularly indebted to Kevin Lee and Doris Schattschneider for their help with the notation system.[1]

The symmetry group of a pattern is the combination of all the operations that are done to a primary cell (translation, rotation, mirror, glide) to create a tile that repeats through translation to produce the pattern, and the notation system tells what each of those operations is. The

1. Kevin Lee is an instructor of computer science at Century College in St. Paul, Minnesota. Doris Schattschneider is a professor of mathematics at Moravian College in Bethlehem, Pennsylvania.

crystallographic system is based on up to four symbols. My interpretation of those symbols is explained below. Many of those symbols have been shortened to produce the standard system that is now most commonly used for describing these symmetries.

Going from left to right on a label, my interpretation is as follows:

1. The first letter in all the groups is either a *p* or a *c*. The *p* stands for the primary cell (the crystallographers call this the primitive cell). The *c* stands for centered cell (I refer to this as a staggered cell), but it is still actually a primary cell.

2. A number in the second position indicates the highest order of rotation that is done in the symmetry. At what point the rotation occurs in the forming of the tile is determined by the letters that follow the number. Any time there is an *m* (indicating mirror) directly following the number it means that the rotation occurs on the mirror line. In other words, the cell must be mirrored first and then rotated along the angle formed by the mirror. If an *m* comes in the fourth position after another letter, the cell must first be rotated and then the mirror applied to the result.

   Symmetry groups that contain only the letter *p* or *c* followed by a number are very straightforward. The notation p1 means that one complete rotation (360°) generates the tile. This is essentially the same as doing nothing to the cell. Any time a *1* occurs in other labels, it is there simply as a placeholder, meaning that no action takes place. The notation p2 means the tile is rotated two times (180°); p3 means it is rotated three times (120°); p4 means the cell is rotated four times (90°); and p6 means the cell is rotated six times (60°). If there is no number in the label, it means that no rotation is necessary to create the tile.

3. The third position (or second if there is no number in the label) is a letter and indicates the first operation that is done to one of the sides of the primary cell (*m* = mirror, g = glide, 1 = no operation prior to rotation).

4. The fourth position (or third if there is no number in the second position of the label) is also a letter and indicates what is done to an adjacent side of the cell.

The following chart shows the crystallographers' labels of the 17 two-dimensional symmetry groups, the shortened standard notation, the name that I have given to the group, and a brief explanation. In the explanation the term *primary cell* has been shortened to *cell*. The description indicates what operations generate the repeating tile.

NOTE: *When there are two ms (mm) in the notation it means that there are both horizontal and vertical mirror lines along a right angle of the cell.*

Two-Dimensional Symmetry Groups

Author Notation	Crystal Notation	Short Version	How to Create the Tile	Symmetry Layout
1. Translation	p1	p1	One 360° rotation repeats the cell, which is also the tile. Essentially nothing has to be done to the cell.	
2. Midpoint or Half-Turn Rotation	p211	p2	The cell is rotated 180° (two times) along the midpoint of one of its sides.	
3. Pinwheel or Quarter-Turn Rotation	p4	p4	The cell is rotated 90° (four times) around one of the corners.	
4. Glide	p1g1	pg	The cell is glided either horizontally, vertically, or diagonally.	
5. Double Glide	p2gg	pgg	The cell is glided two times both horizontally and vertically, or diagonally in two directions.	
6. Mirror	p1m1	pm	The cell is mirrored.	
7. Staggered Mirror	c1m1	cm	The cell is mirrored and then staggered.	
8. Glided Staggered Mirror	p2mg	pmg	The cell is mirrored, staggered, and then glided.	
9. Double Mirror	p2mm	pmm	The cell is mirrored horizontally and vertically along one of the right angles.	

Author Notation	Crystal Notation	Standard Label	How to Create the Tile	Symmetry Layout
10. Staggered Double Mirror	c2mm	cmm	The cell is mirrored horizontally and vertically along one of the right angles and the result is then staggered.	
11. Mirrored Pinwheel	p4gm	p4g	The cell is first rotated four times, then the result is glided (which produces the same result as if it were mirrored, hence "mirrored pinwheel").	
12. Traditional Block	p4mm	p4m	The cell is mirrored and then rotated four times along the angle created by the mirror.	
13. Three Rotation	p3	p3	The cell is rotated three times.	
14. Six Rotation	p6	p6	The cell is rotated six times.	
15. Mirror and Three Rotations	p3m1	p3m1	Because the *m* follows the 3, the cell is first mirrored and then rotated three times along the angle created by the mirror.	
16. Three Rotations and a Mirror	p31m	p31m	Because the *m* is in the fourth position, the cell is first rotated and then mirrored along any one of its sides.	
17. Kaleidoscope	p6mm	p6m	Because an *m* follows the number, the cell is first mirrored then rotated six times along the 60° angle formed by the mirror line.	

The One-Dimensional (Linear) Symmetry Labels

There has been a wide variety of labels attached to the linear symmetry groups. The notations explained in this book are the ones most commonly used.

Each of the linear symmetries has a label made up of two symbols—either two letters, two numbers, or a combination of a letter and a number. The first position will always contain either an *m* or a *1*. If an *m* is in the first position it means that the symmetry will contain vertical mirrors. A *1* in the first position indicates that there are no vertical mirrors and no other changes. The *1*, just as in the two-dimensional symmetries, is used simply as a placeholder.

The symbol in the second position will be either a *1*, *2*, *m*, or *g*. The *1* indicates no change and is there to complete the notation. A *2* indicates midpoint or half-turn rotation, a *g* indicates a glide, and an *m* indicates that a horizontal mirror occurs.

I have attached my own labels to the linear symmetry groups. My notations, along with the now-standard labels are listed in the chart.

At right, vertical and horizontal mirrors.

Vertical mirror (mirror line runs in a vertical direction).

Horizontal mirror (mirror line runs in a horizontal direction).

Dotted line indicates mirror line.

One-Dimensional Symmetry Groups

Author Notation	Standard Label	How to Create the Tile	Symmetry Layout
1. Translation	11	The *1* in both positions indicates that no changes are made to the cell to produce the tile. The cell is the tile.	Γ Γ Γ Γ Γ Γ Γ
2. Midpoint Rotation	12	The *1* indicates no vertical mirrors and the 2 indicates 180° rotation.	Γ J Γ J Γ J Γ J
3. Glide	1g	The *1* indicates no vertical mirrors and the *g* indicates a glide reflection.	Γ L Γ L Γ L Γ L
4. Vertical Mirror	m1	The *m* in the first position indicates a vertical mirror and the *1* shows no other changes.	Γ ⅂ Γ ⅂ Γ ⅂ Γ ⅂
5. Horizontal Mirror	1m	The *1* in the first position indicates no vertical mirrors, but the *m* in the second position indicates horizontal mirrors.	Γ Γ Γ Γ Γ Γ Γ L L L L L L L
6. Glided Mirror	mg	The *m* in the first position indicates vertical mirrors, and the *g* in the second position indicates that those mirrors are then glided.	Γ ⅂ L J Γ ⅂ L J
7. Double Mirror	mm	The double *m* indicates that there are both vertical and horizontal mirrors.	Γ ⅂ Γ ⅂ Γ ⅂ Γ ⅂ L J L J L J L J

Aurora, *Jinny Beyer*, 1989.
Four large units are rotated for the design of this quilt. It is an example of pinwheel (p4) symmetry.

CHAPTER 3

Designing with Two-Dimensional Symmetries:
The First Eleven Symmetry Groups

THE FIRST 11 SYMMETRY GROUPS are best explained using a square primary cell. Some patterns can also be generated with other shapes. Those shapes will be discussed later, but for simplicity the square is used for the illustrations and exercises. In order for you to see how different the motif can look depending on the symmetry operation applied, the same primary cell has been used in the explanation of all of these first 11 symmetry groups.

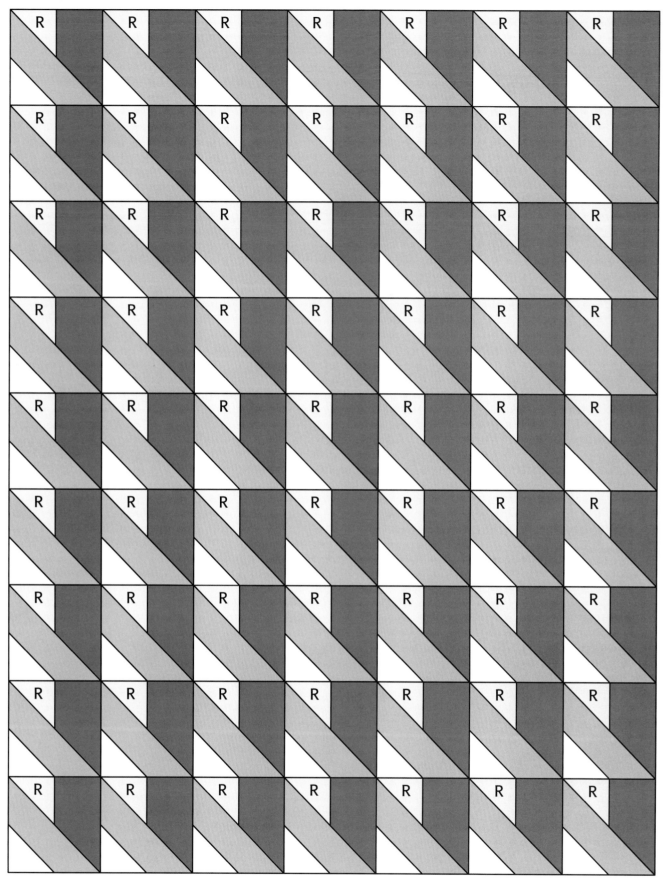

Illustration 3.1. Cell page. Photocopy this page onto plain paper and acetate to use for experimenting with the first 11 symmetries.

Working with Symmetries

The next two chapters describe in detail how to create patterns from a primary cell by manipulating it in a variety of ways. Looking at the illustrations and reading does not necessarily cement the concepts of how to generate symmetrical patterns. I did not fully understand the symmetry groups until I sat and worked with primary cells and arranged patterns in each of the groups. The easiest way for you to learn is to move and arrange the cells yourself, and I recommend you do each of the exercises in these chapters.

Photocopy the cell pages shown in Illustrations 3.1 and 4.1. Make one photocopy of each page on plain paper to use for the first three symmetry groups (these do not require a mirror image to create the tile), and photocopy each page again on clear acetate for those symmetry groups that will require a reverse of the cell. The letter *R* is on the cell so that you can see when the cell is right side up and when it is reversed.

To create patterns in each of the symmetry groups, begin by cutting out individual primary cells and taping two or more of those cells together to create a tile. Then make several identical tiles and orient the tiles in the same direction. Place the tiles side by side to form the pattern.

Patterns in the first 11 symmetry groups are explained in this chapter and can be formed by using the primary cell sheet shown here. The last six symmetry groups, explained in Chapter 4, will require different primary cells and those can be found on pages 68 and 69. Keep your results in a notebook that you can use as a guide for reference purposes. Indicate the primary cell, show a separate tile and then show several tiles placed side by side. Label each of the layouts and indicate whether it required a reversed version of the cell.

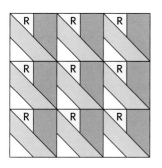

Primary cell   Multiple tiles placed side by side and
and tile   oriented in same direction

Illustration 3.2. Translation symmetry.

1. Translation (p1) Symmetry

Patterns in the first symmetry group are the easiest. In translation the primary cell is the tile and that cell or tile is repeated over and over by translation. The tiles are always oriented in the same direction and are moved sideways and up and down. The words *mama* and *papa* are examples of translation symmetry as there is one syllable that repeats exactly to form the pattern of the word.

Illustration 3.2 shows the primary cell translated side by side and is an example of translation (p1) symmetry. The *Yellow Houses* quilt on page 12 is another example.

It can sometimes be confusing to analyze patterns and to understand where the primary cell and tiles or translation units are. In fact when looking at an allover design, such as commonly found in many fabrics, any number of different sections could be thought of as a tile. The main consideration is to find an area that contains all parts of the design that will repeat over and over to produce the pattern.

We tend to see a particular motif and want to think of that as the tile, but in fact the tile might contain only parts of the motif, and when the tiles go together those parts join to create the entire motif once again. One of the easiest ways to find the repeat of the design is to draw lines connecting the places where adjacent motifs meet, creating a grid across the surface of the design, as in the case of Escher's birds (Illustration 3.3). Alternatively, draw lines from some part of a motif to the same part of an adjacent motif, as in the case of the fabric design shown in Illustration 3.4.

Standard Notation—p1

I find it easiest to call this first symmetry "translation," but for those who wish to refer to it as "p1," my interpretation of the standard notation labeling system is as follows. The *p* refers to the primary cell, and the number after the *p* can be interpreted in two ways. First the *1* can refer to the number of rotations that are applied to the cell to generate the pattern. In this case the *1* means that the primary cell (p) is rotated one (1) full turn or 360° to create the pattern. So in essence it simply rotates back to itself. Thus one cell creates the tile and that single cell or tile is translated for the pattern. The other interpretation of the *1* is simply to refer to it as a placeholder because no operation is necessary to create the tile.

Illustration 3.3. Symmetry Drawing E128 by M. C. Escher.

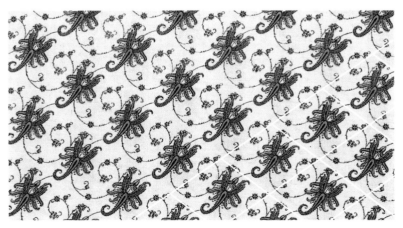

Illustration 3.4. Fabric design showing translation (p1) symmetry.

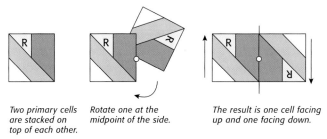

Two primary cells are stacked on top of each other.

Rotate one at the midpoint of the side.

The result is one cell facing up and one facing down.

Illustration 3.5. Creating the tile for midpoint rotation symmetry.

2. Midpoint or Half-Turn Rotation (p2) Symmetry

Two primary cells are required to create the tile for designs in the midpoint or half-turn rotation (p2) symmetry group. To see how this symmetry group works, cut two of the primary cells from your photocopies of page 32, and stack them on top of each other. Now place a pin at the midpoint of a side and rotate the top one 180°. What you will have is one cell pointing up and another one pointing down as shown in Illustration 3.5.

Create sets of tiles and then put the tiles together by translation. Three different patterns can be generated from this symmetry, depending on whether the side of the cell, the bottom, or both the side and the bottom are midpoint rotated. (The same overall pattern will occur whether you midpoint rotate the right side of the cell or the left side, as in Illustration 3.6a. Likewise for the second pattern; you will get the same design by rotating

Standard Notation—p2

The p2 designation of this symmetry can be interpreted as the primary cell (p) rotated 180° (2) at the midpoint of a side. In p1 the cell used the entire 360°. In p2, the cell uses half the degrees, or 180°, thus requiring two cells to make a full 360°, or to create the tile.

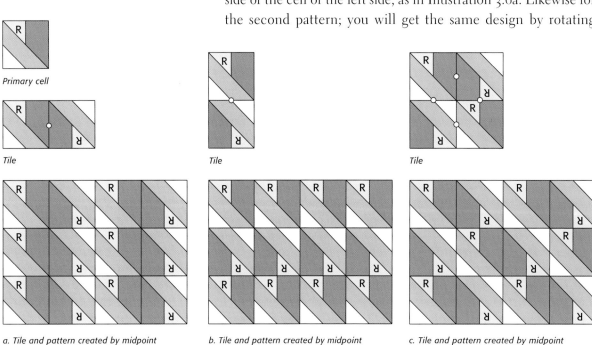

Primary cell

Tile

Tile

Tile

a. Tile and pattern created by midpoint rotating the side of the cell

b. Tile and pattern created by midpoint rotating the bottom of the cell

c. Tile and pattern created by midpoint rotating all sides of the cell

Illustration 3.6. Examples of three variations of midpoint rotation (p2) symmetry.

Illustration 3.7. Examples of midpoint rotation symmetry. The dot indicates where the rotation occurs.

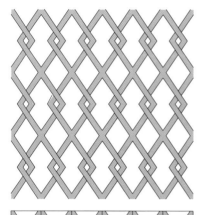

Illustration 3.8. The jack of clubs is an example of midpoint rotation (p2) symmetry.

either the top or bottom of the cell, as in Illustration 3.6b.) A third pattern can be made by double midpoint rotating. This requires four primary cells. Once the side of the cell has been midpoint rotated, midpoint rotate the bottoms of each of those cells (Illustration 3.6c).

The capital letters N, Z, and S are examples of midpoint rotation symmetry. You will see that if you cut one of the letters in half, draw one of the halves onto tracing paper, and then rotate the paper by 180°, that half will exactly fit with the other half. The same is true with the word *pod*. If the word is split in half vertically through the *o*, you will see that when one half is rotated by 180° the two halves are identical (Illustration 3.7).

I remember as a child how fascinated I was with the jack, queen, and king in a deck of cards. I couldn't quite figure out how anyone could create a design and know that when you turned the card upside down the faces staring at you would be exactly the same. But when the card is cut in half, you can see that the two halves are exactly the same, one half is simply rotated 180° at the midpoint (Illustration 3.8).

An interlaced lattice or chain-link fence is also a midpoint rotation symmetry. Looking at the design it is very difficult to see how the pattern is generated, but if common points are connected to create a grid across the design, it soon becomes apparent how the pattern is produced as shown in Illustration 3.9. Other examples of midpoint rotation (p2) are shown in Illustrations 3.10 to 3.12.

 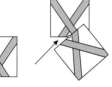

Primary cell   Two primary cells rotated 180° at the midpoint of a side   Tile

Illustration 3.9. An intertwined lattice pattern can at first be confusing, but when the grid is placed on top, the primary cell can be isolated.

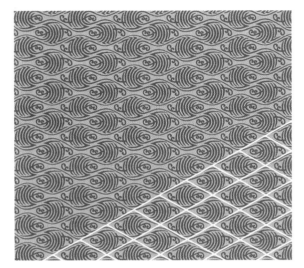

Illustration 3.10. The pattern in this fabric is an example of midpoint rotation (p2) symmetry. The underlying grid is a parallelogram.

Illustration 3.11. This window found on a downtown street in Kathmandu, Nepal, is another example of midpoint rotation (p2) symmetry.

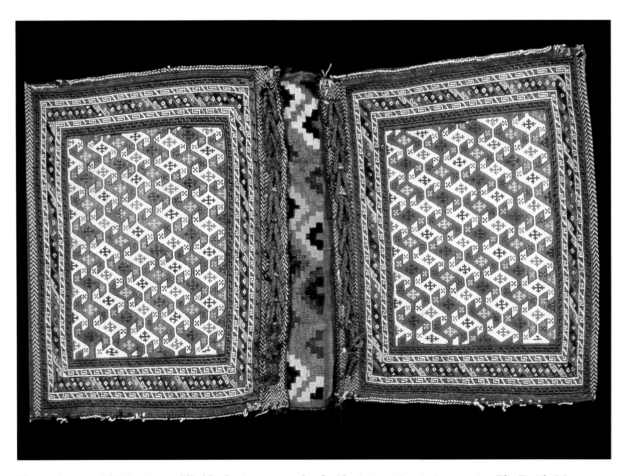

Illustration 3.12. This Iranian saddle blanket is an example of midpoint rotation (p2) symmetry. The Textile Museum, Washington, D. C. No. 1961.39.5. Gift of Arthur D. Jenkins.

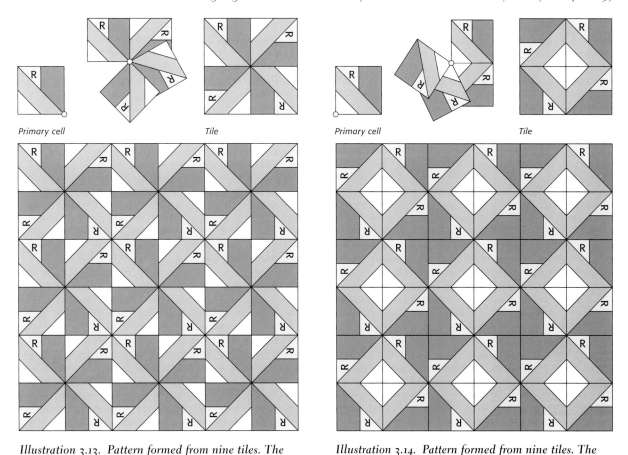

Illustration 3.13. Pattern formed from nine tiles. The primary cell is rotated around lower right corner.

Illustration 3.14. Pattern formed from nine tiles. The primary cell is rotated around lower left corner.

3. Pinwheel or Quarter-Turn (p4) Symmetry

Four cells are required to create the tile for patterns in the pinwheel (p4) symmetry group. Stack four primary cells on top of each other making sure they are oriented in the same direction. Put a pin in one of the corners and rotate the first three by 90°, then the top two by 90°, and finally the top one by 90° until they all come together spinning around that corner to form the tile.

Two different patterns can be generated with a primary cell in this symmetry group depending on which corner is rotated. One pattern is created if the upper right or lower left corners are rotated, and a different pattern occurs if the upper left or lower right corners are rotated. However, a note of clarification should be made. A different tile will occur if the lower right and upper left corners are rotated, but when the tiles are repeated the same patterns occur. The same is true with rotating the upper right and lower left corners.

Illustrations 3.15 and 3.16 show several examples of pinwheel (p4) symmetry. *Row Houses* on page 41 and *Aurora* on page 30 are also good examples.

Standard Notation—p4

The p4 designation of this symmetry can be interpreted as the primary cell (p) rotated four (4) times around one of the corners. I see a pinwheel very readily in this symmetry and prefer to call it pinwheel symmetry.

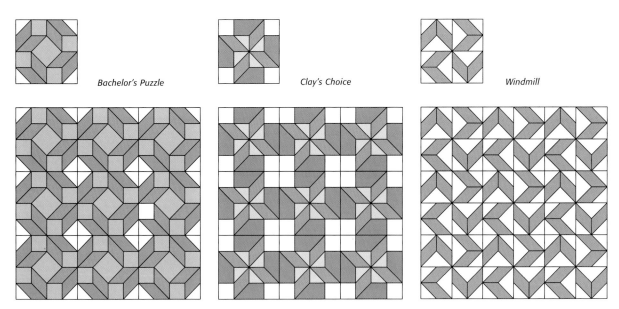

Bachelor's Puzzle   Clay's Choice   Windmill

Illustration 3.15. Examples of pinwheel (p4) symmetry in traditional-style quilt patterns.

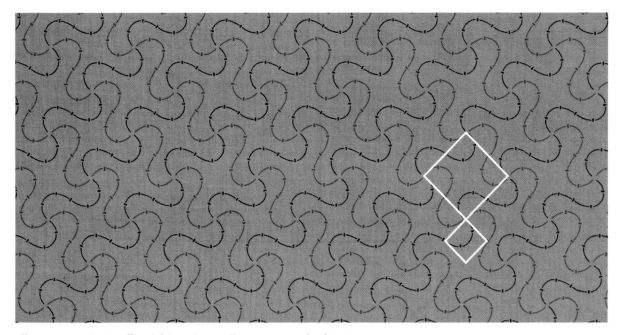

Illustration 3.16. Tessellated fabric design illustrating pinwheel (p4) symmetry.

Row Houses, *Judy Spahn, 1983.*
An example of pinwheel (p4) symmetry, the center portion of this quilt
contains four units of house blocks, each unit containing four houses
rotated around their chimneys. Single rows of houses run across the top
and bottom of the quilt.

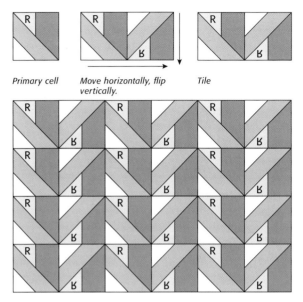

Primary cell   Move horizontally, flip   Tile
                vertically.

Illustration 3.17. One pattern of glide (pg) symmetry is formed when the primary cell is moved horizontally and flipped vertically.

Illustration 3.18. Rows of zippers show glide (pg) symmetry.

Standard Notation—pg

The pg name for this symmetry refers to the primary cell (p) with a glide reflection (g). I find it easiest to call it a glide.

4. Glide (pg) Symmetry

The three symmetry groups that have been discussed so far all involve the rotation of the primary cell with no flipping. The next eight symmetry groups require that the primary cell be flipped, or turned upside down. Therefore, since half of the cells for each tile will be reversed, you will need to work with a clear acetate photocopy of the cells.

Two cells are required to make up the tile for patterns in the glide (pg) symmetry group. To create the tile, stack two of the cells on top of each other, both right side up and oriented in the same direction. Now take the top cell and move it over to the right (horizontally), then flip the cell upside down (vertically). This is a glide (Illustration 3.17). When the tiles are put together you will see that you have vertical rows, the first row with all the tiles oriented in the same direction and the next row with the tiles flipped. Imagine rows of zippers side by side and you get a similar type of pattern (Illustration 3.18).

Four different patterns can be created with a glide, depending on which way the glide is performed. For example, the pattern in Illustration 3.17 is created by moving the cell horizontally (sideways) and flipping it vertically, but a different pattern is formed if the cell is moved down (vertically) and then flipped

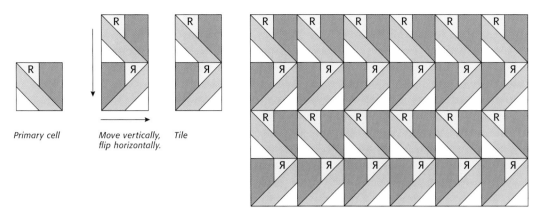

Illustration 3.19. Glide pattern formed by moving the cell vertically and flipping horizontally.

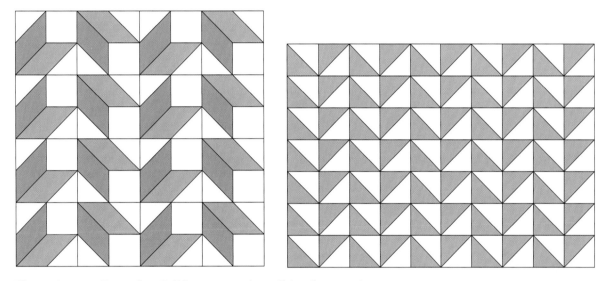

Illustration 3.20. Examples of glide symmetry, in traditional geometric patterns.

horizontally (Illustration 3.19). The main point to remember when generating a glide is that if the cell is moved horizontally, it is flipped vertically. Conversely, if the cell is moved vertically, it is flipped horizontally. Two patterns not shown here can also be created by diagonally gliding the primary cell. (See page 21.) Illustrations 3.20 through 3.22 depict other patterns that have been created with glide symmetry. *Chorus Line Choreography* exemplifies glide symmetry where a cell was first moved horizontally and then flipped vertically. Illustration 3.22 shows how the pattern was created.

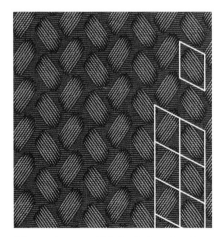

Illustration 3.21. Fabric design showing an example of glide (pg) symmetry.

Chorus Line Choreography, *Carole Nicholas, 1997, from the collection of Kay and David McClain.*
This is one of several quilts made by members of the staff of an annual seminar run by Jinny Beyer at Hilton Head, South Carolina. The challenge was to use the same primary cell to illustrate various symmetries. The cell chosen is from a quilt block design named Discovery. The quilts shown on pages 49, 52, 56, 61, and 64 all use this same primary cell.

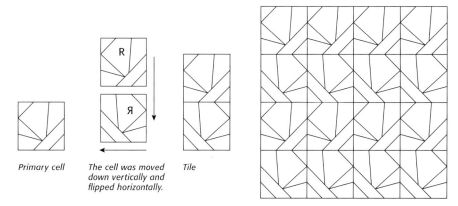

Primary cell   The cell was moved   Tile
                      down vertically and
                      flipped horizontally.

Illustration 3.22. Diagram of Chorus Line Choreography *by Carole Nicholas.*

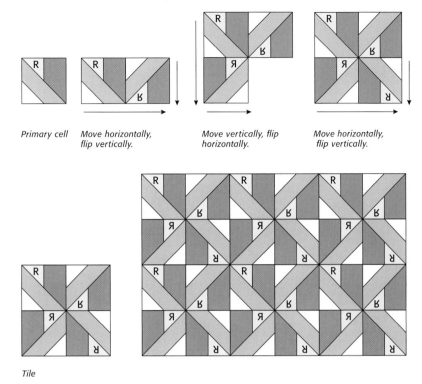

Illustration 3.23. Double glide (pgg) symmetry.

Standard Notation—pgg

The pgg label refers to the primary cell (p) with two glides (gg). Crystallographers keep a 2 in the notation (p2gg). My interpretation of this notation is the primary cell (p) with two glides (gg) and rotated 180° (2). To understand how the tile is generated with this notation, create two horizontally glided tiles and stack them on top of each other oriented in the same direction. Now place a pin at the bottom in between the two tiles and rotate the top one 180° around to the bottom. You will see that this is another way to generate the double glide tile, as this tile is exactly the same as the one shown opposite.

5. Double Glide (pgg) Symmetry

Four cells are required to make up the tile for double glide (pgg) symmetry. Cut out four of the primary cells from the acetate and stack two of them on top of each other, right side up and oriented in the same direction. Do a horizontal glide (move the top cell horizontally and flip it vertically). Take another of the cells and place it on top of the first cell (the one in the upper left corner) oriented in the same direction, and this time do a vertical glide (slide the cell down vertically and flip it horizontally). Finally place the last cell on top of the one you just glided (the one in the lower left corner). Make sure that it is in exactly the same position as the cell it is placed upon. Now glide that cell to the right to fill the last hole. (Move it horizontally and flip it vertically.)

Examples of double glide (pgg) symmetry are shown in Illustrations 3.24 and 3.25, as well as in the quilt *Cottage Garden Fan* on page 46. Two other double glide (pgg) patterns not shown here can be created using diagonal glides. (See page 21.)

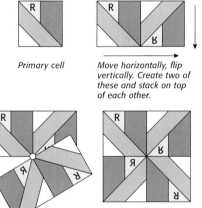

Illustration 3.24. Alternate way of creating the tile for the double glide (pgg) symmetry.

Primary cell

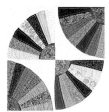

Tile

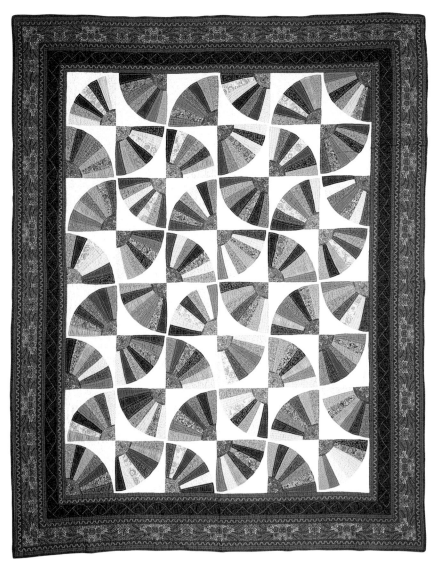

Cottage Garden Fan, *Robin Morrison, 1998. The pattern of this quilt is an example of double glide (pgg) symmetry.*

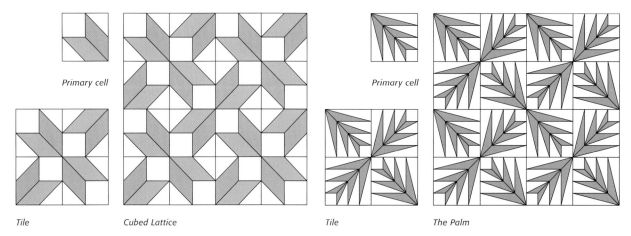

Primary cell   *Primary cell*

Tile   *Cubed Lattice*   *Tile*   *The Palm*

Illustration 3.25. Examples of double glide (pgg) symmetry in traditional-style quilt patterns.

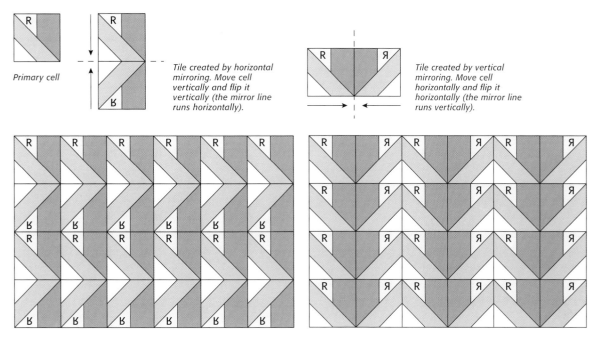

Primary cell

Tile created by horizontal mirroring. Move cell vertically and flip it vertically (the mirror line runs horizontally).

Tile created by vertical mirroring. Move cell horizontally and flip it horizontally (the mirror line runs vertically).

Pattern created with horizontally mirrored tile

Pattern created with vertically mirrored tile

Illustration 3.26. Mirror (pm) symmetry.

6. Mirror (pm) Symmetry

Two cells are required to make the tile for patterns in the mirror (pm) symmetry group. Cut out two of the cells from acetate and stack them right side up, one on top of the other, making sure they are both oriented the same. The *R* on the cell indicates the right side. Place a mirror along one side of the cell to see what a mirror image of the motif looks like.

To create the tile pretend you are opening the back cover of a book. Pick up the top cell and open it out. Tape the two cells together for the tile. In reality the cell is moved horizontally and then flipped horizontally. Make several tiles and then put the tiles together by translation, one after the other. Creating the mirror tile is very similar to creating the glided tile, with one very important difference. In a glide if the cell is moved horizontally it is flipped vertically, and with a mirror if it is moved horizontally it is also flipped horizontally, thus one cell is the exact mirror image of the other.

Standard Notation—pm

In the standard notation labeling system, *pm* stands for the primary cell (p), which is mirrored (m).

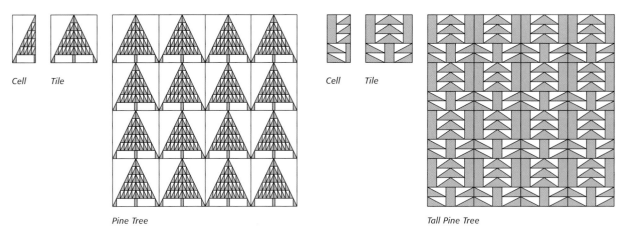

Cell   *Tile*   *Pine Tree*   *Cell*   *Tile*   *Tall Pine Tree*

Illustration 3.27. *Examples of mirror symmetry in traditional-style quilt patterns.*

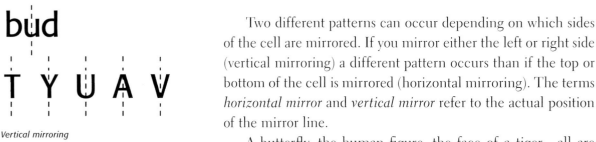

Vertical mirroring

Horizontal mirroring

Illustration 3.28. *Examples of vertical and horizontal mirroring.*

Two different patterns can occur depending on which sides of the cell are mirrored. If you mirror either the left or right side (vertical mirroring) a different pattern occurs than if the top or bottom of the cell is mirrored (horizontal mirroring). The terms *horizontal mirror* and *vertical mirror* refer to the actual position of the mirror line.

A butterfly, the human figure, the face of a tiger—all are examples of mirror symmetry. The capital letters *T, Y, U, A, V,* and *M* and the word *bud* are examples of vertical mirroring. The letters *E, D, K, C,* and *B* are examples of horizontal mirroring. Illustrations 3.27 to 3.31 show examples of designs that have been created by means of mirror (pm) symmetry.

Illustration 3.29. *Fabric with mirror (pm) symmetry. The cell is a rectangle.*

Illustration 3.30. *Two sleeping dogs form almost perfect mirror symmetry on a symmetrically placed tile floor.*

Twist Me and Turn Me, *Paula Golden, 1997. An example of mirror (pm) symmetry, this is another seminar challenge quilt that uses the* Discovery *primary cell. See also the quilts on pages 44, 52, 56, 61, and 64.*

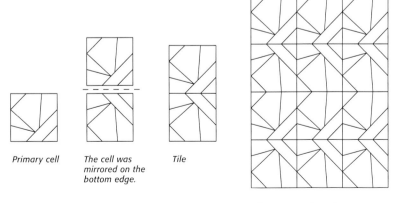

Primary cell

The cell was mirrored on the bottom edge.

Tile

Tiles repeat to form the pattern.

Illustration 3.31. Twist Me and Turn Me *by Paula Golden is an example of mirror (pm) symmetry.*

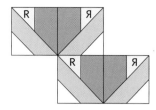
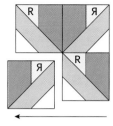
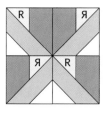

Primary cell   *Horizontal mirrors staggered*   *Move the cell straight over to fill the hole.*   *Tile created with horizontally staggered mirrors*

Standard Notation—cm

In the standard notation label for this symmetry *c* stands for "centered" cell and *m* stands for mirror. I just feel that staggered mirrors is easy to see and also to remember.

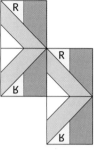
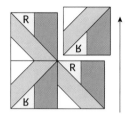
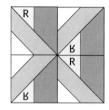

Vertical mirrors staggered   *Move the cell straight up to fill the hole.*   *Tile created with vertically staggered mirrors*

Illustration 3.32. Two different tiles can be created with staggered mirror (cm) symmetry and they each produce different patterns.

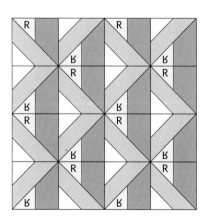

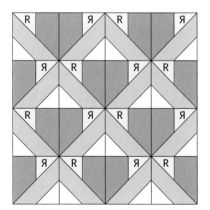

Illustration 3.33. Patterns formed from the two tiles created by staggered mirror (cm) symmetry.

7. Staggered Mirror (cm) Symmetry

The staggered mirror (cm) symmetry group is very similar to the mirror (pm) symmetry group, the only difference being that the mirrored cells are staggered when put together, instead of lined up one on top of the other. Four primary cells are needed to create the tile for patterns in this symmetry group.

To generate the tile, make two mirrored tiles just as you did in the mirror (pm) symmetry group. Now stagger the tiles as shown in Illustration 3.32. This staggered group of cells could actually be used for the tiles, as the units would continually fit together to form the pattern, but it would be awkward to work with. It is easier to work with a square tile. To create the square tile, pick up the cell that sticks out on the bottom right and move it over to fill in the hole on the left.

Just as in the mirror symmetry group, two completely different patterns occur depending on whether the cell is mirrored on one of the two sides and then staggered, or whether it is mirrored on the top or bottom and then staggered.

Patterns in the staggered mirror (cm) symmetry group are interesting in that two different cells, a square and a triangle, can be used to generate the same design. In fact the primary cells of

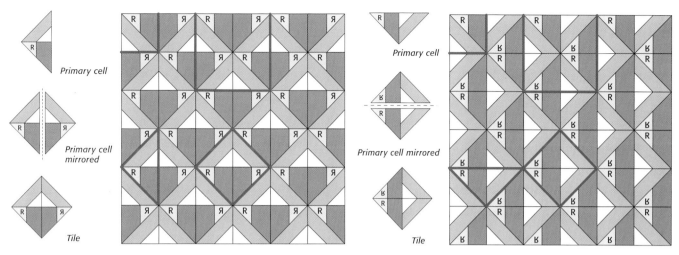

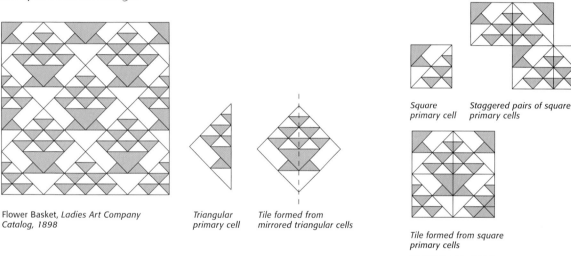

Illustration 3.34. Staggered mirror (cm) symmetry with triangular primary cell. The same pattern is generated from both the square and the triangle cells. The red lines in the illustrations indicate the primary cells and the tiles for both the square and the triangle.

Flower Basket, *Ladies Art Company Catalog, 1898*

Triangular primary cell

Tile formed from mirrored triangular cells

Square primary cell

Staggered pairs of square primary cells

Tile formed from square primary cells

many of the patterns that contain this type of symmetry are more readily apparent in the triangular shape than in the square. For instance look again at the pattern created with the primary cell and you will begin to see, not the mirrored square cells, but a diagonally set square composed of two mirrored triangles. Both cells produce the same pattern. Red lines in Illustrations 3.34 indicate the square cell and tile and the triangular cell and tile.

The quilt *Garden Reflections* is an example of the staggered mirror (cm) symmetry group. The traditional *Flower Basket* patchwork design is also an example of the staggered mirror symmetry group, and one where the mirrored triangles are readily apparent. If you study this type of design carefully, however, you will also find a mirrored square cell that has been staggered, as shown in Illustrations 3.35 through 3.38.

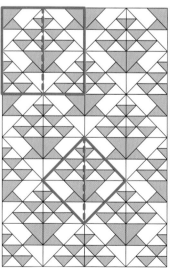

Illustration 3.35. Flower Basket design showing tiles formed from both triangular and square primary cells.

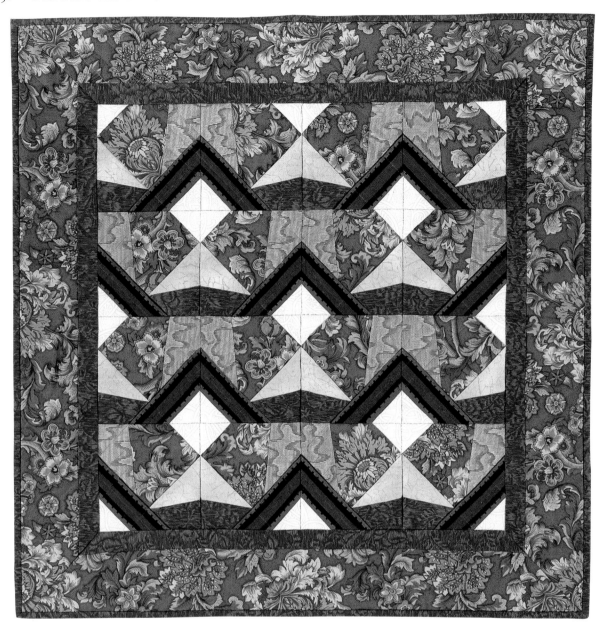

Garden Reflections, *Kaye Rhodes, 1997. This quilt uses the identical primary cell,
Discovery, as the quilts shown on pages 44, 49, 56, 61, and 64, illustrating the diversity
of design that can occur with simply a change of symmetry and contrasts.*

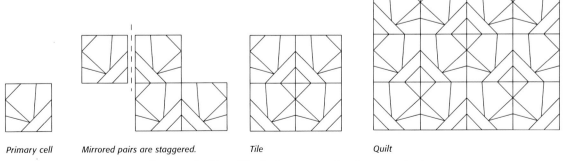

Primary cell   *Mirrored pairs are staggered.*   *Tile*   *Quilt*

Illustration 3.36. Garden Reflections *by Kaye Rhodes is an example of staggered mirror (cm) symmetry.*

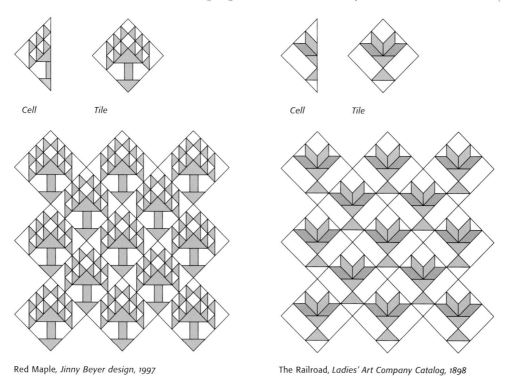

Cell   Tile   Cell   Tile

Red Maple, *Jinny Beyer design, 1997*   The Railroad, *Ladies' Art Company Catalog, 1898*

Illustration 3.37. Examples of staggered mirror (cm) symmetry in traditional style quilt patterns.

Illustration 3.38. Fabric designs showing examples of staggered mirror (cm) symmetry.

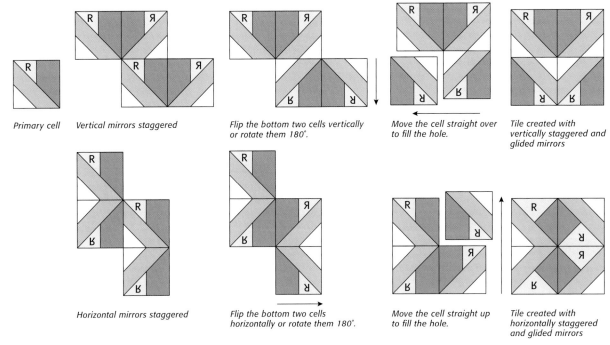

Primary cell   *Vertical mirrors staggered*

Flip the bottom two cells vertically or rotate them 180°.

Move the cell straight over to fill the hole.

Tile created with vertically staggered and glided mirrors

Horizontal mirrors staggered

Flip the bottom two cells horizontally or rotate them 180°.

Move the cell straight up to fill the hole.

Tile created with horizontally staggered and glided mirrors

Illustration 3.39. Two different tiles created from the same cell with glided staggered mirror (pmg) symmetry.

Standard Notation—pmg

In the labeling system *pmg* stands for the primary cell (p), which is first mirrored (m) and then glided (g).

8. Glided Staggered Mirror (pmg) Symmetry

The glided staggered mirror (pmg) symmetry group is almost identical to the staggered mirror group, with one major difference. When one set of mirrors is staggered from the other as in staggered mirror (cm), that set is also flipped upside down. To create the tile, make two sets of mirrored cells, just as in the two previous symmetry groups. Stagger one set of mirrors, then either flip it vertically or rotate it 180°. To create a square tile, pick up the cell that protrudes on the right and move it over to fill the hole on the left. You can create two different patterns depending on which side of the primary cell is mirrored. Illustration 3.39 shows the two possibilities and how to make the tiles. Compare these with the staggered mirror symmetry group in Illustration 3.32 on page 50.

The quilt *Challenge* (page 56) is a good example of the glided staggered mirror (pmg) symmetry group. The examples in Illustrations 3.40 and 3.41 also show patterns in the glided staggered mirror (pmg) symmetry group.

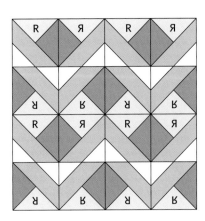
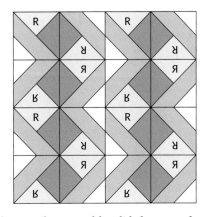

Illustration 3.40. Patterns formed by the two tiles created by glided staggered mirror (pmg) symmetry.

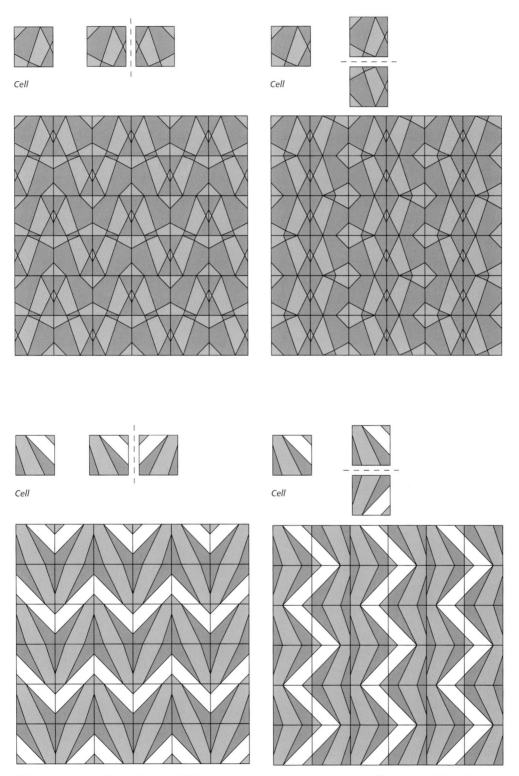

Cell

Cell

Cell

Cell

Illustration 3.41. Examples of glided staggered mirror (pmg) symmetry. The same cell has been used for each set of designs. The difference in the designs is based on which side of the cell was mirrored.

Challenge, *Laura Chapman, 1997. This quilt uses the identical primary cell, Discovery, as the quilts shown on pages 44, 49, 52, 61, and 64. This quilt illustrates once again the diversity of design that can occur with a simple change of symmetry and contrasts.*

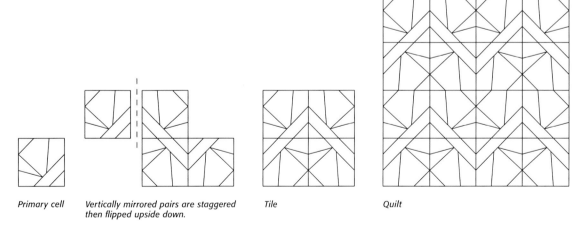

Primary cell   Vertically mirrored pairs are staggered then flipped upside down.   Tile   Quilt

Illustration 3.42. Challenge by Laura Chapman is an example of glided staggered mirror (pmg) symmetry.

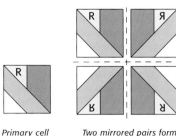

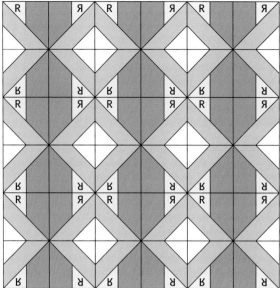

Primary cell   Two mirrored pairs form
the tile. One pair is the
mirror image of the other.

Illustration 3.43. Double mirror (pmm) symmetry.

9. Double Mirror (pmm) Symmetry

Four primary cells are required to create the tile for the double mirror (pmm) symmetry group. Place mirrors on all four sides of one primary cell and then look into them to see what the pattern generated by the symmetry group looks like. To create the tile, make two sets of mirrored pairs. Stack them on top of each other, oriented in the same direction. Then simply move the cells straight down and flip them vertically.

Blue Star Sapphire on page 58 uses double mirror (pmm) symmetry. The letter X is an example of double mirror symmetry. Other examples are shown in Illustrations 3.44 and 3.45.

Standard Notation—pmm

In the labeling system for this symmetry, *p* stands for primary cell, and *mm* means there is both a horizontal and vertical mirror along a right angle.

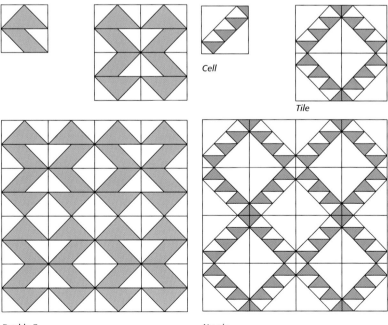

Cell

Tile

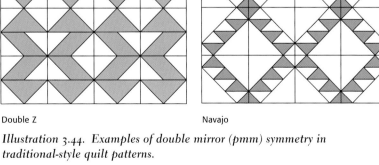

Double Z   Navajo

Illustration 3.44. Examples of double mirror (pmm) symmetry in traditional-style quilt patterns.

Illustration 3.45. Fabric design showing example of double mirror (pmm) symmetry.

Blue Star Sapphire, *Jinny Beyer, 1983. If this quilt is broken down into four large quarter sections, the double mirror (pmm) symmetry is apparent.*

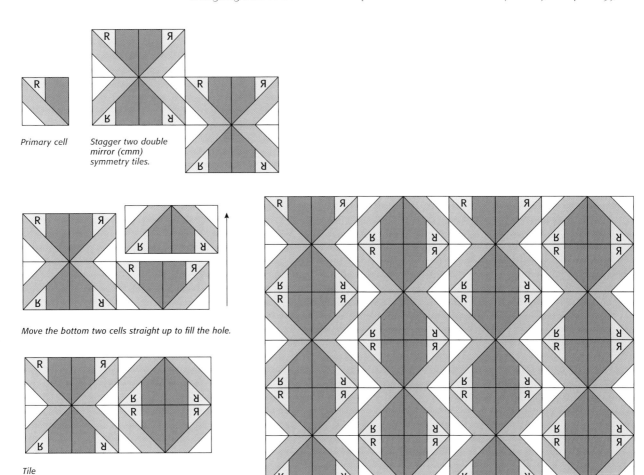

Illustration 3.46. Staggered double mirror (cmm) symmetry.

10. Staggered Double Mirror (cmm) Symmetry

Staggered double mirror (cmm) symmetry is very interesting and patterns in this group can be very dynamic. Eight square cells make up the tile and four different patterns can result depending on how the cell is turned. Begin by making two double mirror tiles (see the symmetry instructions on page 57), then stagger those tiles as shown in Illustration 3.46. Just as in the staggered mirror and staggered glided mirror symmetry groups, it is difficult to work with an odd-shaped tile. Therefore square it off into a rectangle by taking the bottom right two cells and moving them directly upward to fill in the hole.

Standard Notation—cmm

It is easiest to think of the labeling system for this symmetry group as based on the triangle as the primary cell. This triangle produces a tile that covers the smallest area. The c stands for "centered cell" and the first *m* indicates a mirror on one of the sides adjacent to the right angle and the second *m* indicates the resulting triangle is mirrored along its longest side.

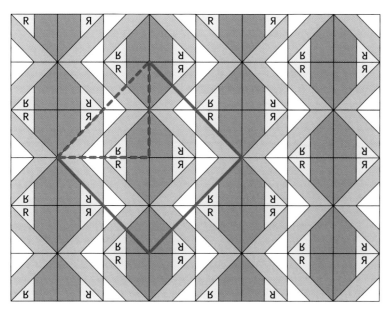

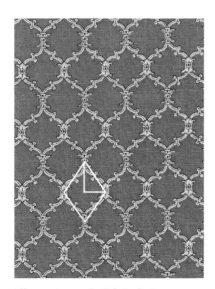

Illustration 3.47. Triangular cell that can be used with staggered double mirror (cmm) symmetry.

Illustration 3.48. Fabric design showing example of staggered double mirror (cmm) symmetry.

Just as in the staggered mirror (cm) symmetry group, a triangular cell can also be used to generate patterns in this symmetry group. This triangle must be a right triangle. The pattern in Illustration 3.46 shows both the square and triangular cell that produce this pattern, with dotted lines. To create the tile, the triangle is double mirrored on the two sides that form the right angle. Both cells, the square one and the triangular one, produce the same pattern.

The quilt *Desert Rose* is an example of staggered double mirror (cmm) symmetry, as is Illustration 3.48. It is very easy to generate patterns using the staggered double mirror symmetry, but when analyzing certain designs the primary cell and the tile are sometimes difficult to discern.

Because the cell can be double mirrored along the sides, adjacent to each of the four corners, four different sets of cells result. If these were the tile as in the double mirror symmetry group they would all produce the same patterns, but since the double mirrors are staggered, each results in a different pattern.

Desert Rose, *Bunnie Jordan, 1997. This quilt uses the same primary cell as other quilts on pages 44, 49, 52, 56, and 64. Here, it is an example of staggered double mirror (cmm) symmetry.*

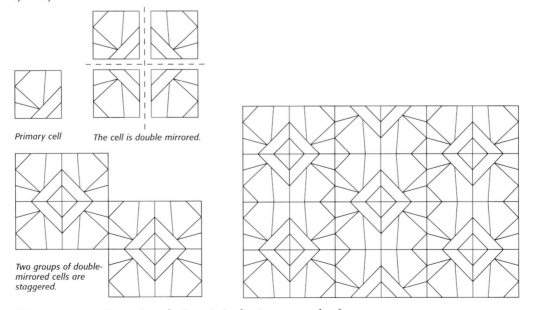

Primary cell   The cell is double mirrored.

Two groups of double-mirrored cells are staggered.

Illustration 3.49. Desert Rose by Bunnie Jordan is an example of staggered double mirror (cmm) symmetry.

Standard Notation—p4g

There are various ways to move a cell to achieve the same pattern. The labeling system for this symmetry appears to be based on the triangle as the primary cell. The cell is first rotated four times around the right angle (p4), that result is then glided (g), which produces the same result as if a square cell was rotated four times and then mirrored.

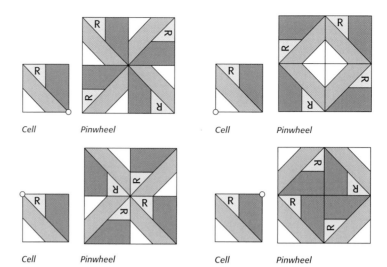

Illustration 3.50. Each of the four corners of the primary cell can be rotated to produce four different pinwheel blocks. Place mirrors on all sides of the pinwheel tiles to see what the mirrored pinwheel (p4g) symmetry pattern looks like.

11. Four Rotations Mirrored or Mirrored Pinwheel (p4g) Symmetry

The third symmetry group, pinwheel (p4), involves rotating the primary cell four times around one of the corners; thus four cells make up the tile. A total of 16 cells is required to make the tile for the mirrored pinwheel (p4g) symmetry, eight of them right side up and eight of them reversed.

To create a pattern in the mirrored pinwheel (p4g) symmetry group begin with a pinwheel tile (see page 39), but then mirror that unit on all sides. In the pinwheel (p4) symmetry group you saw how two different patterns were generated depending on which corners were rotated. The same holds true with patterns in the mirrored pinwheel (p4g) symmetry group, except this time four different patterns can be generated by rotating each of the four corners. You can begin with any of the four pinwheel tiles. Mirror all sides and come up with four different designs, as shown in Illustration 3.52. Two pinwheels and two reversed or mirrored pinwheels are required to make the repeating tile. With the cells photocopied onto acetate, create four pinwheel tiles, all right side up. Now flip two of them over and alternate them as in Illustration 3.51.

To see what the pattern will look like, place two mirrors at right angles along two of the sides of the pinwheel tile.

In the staggered mirror (cm) and the staggered double mirror (cmm) symmetry groups you saw how the same pattern

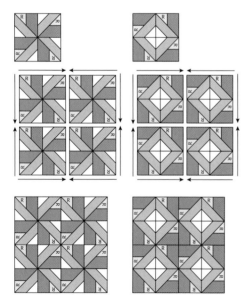

Illustration 3.51. Two of the four tiles that can be created from the primary cell. Dotted lines indicate mirror lines.

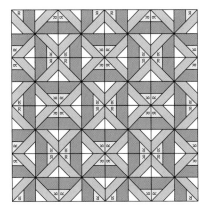 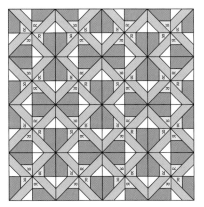 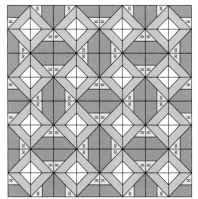

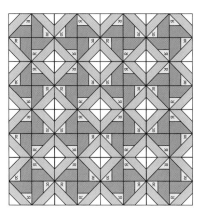

could be generated from two different primary cells, one a square and the other a triangle. The same is true of mirrored pinwheel (p4g) patterns. Depending on the design and how it is going to be used, this triangular cell may be more efficient, since the tile that repeats is smaller and requires fewer cells. In either case whether the square cell or triangular cell is isolated, the pattern is the same.

Two variations of the mirrored pinwheel (p4g) pattern have been repeated in Illustration 3.55. The lines outside the designs show the four tiles, each made up of 16 square cells, that repeat to form the overall pattern. The red lines inside the patterns indicate smaller diagonally set square tiles, but it is apparent that these squares also repeat to form the same pattern.

A breakdown of the smaller diagonally set square tile shows that it is composed of eight triangular cells, four of them right side up and four of them reversed. To generate the pattern, one triangular cell is mirrored and the resulting square is rotated four times on the corner opposite the mirrored side.

The patterns in *Spindown* and *Infinity* (see page 154), as well as the fabric shown here are all examples of mirrored pinwheel (p4g) symmetry. The easiest way to analyze such designs is to first locate the places where the cells have been mirrored. Draw lines directly down the middle of the mirrored pieces, then find the place where the design pinwheels or rotates and draw a line from the center of one rotated group to another. Connect these rotated centers in both directions. Once these lines have been drawn, you should be able to locate either the square cell or the triangular cell, both of which repeat in the manner explained above to create the pattern. In all cases with this symmetry, if it is a triangular cell, the angles must be 90°, 45°, 45°.

Illustration 3.52. Examples of four patterns that can be created with mirrored pinwheel (p4g) symmetry.

Illustration 3.53. Fabric design showing example of mirrored pinwheel (p4g) symmetry.

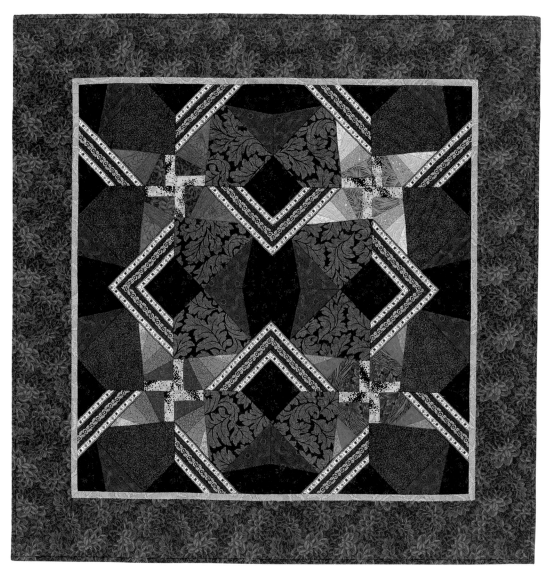

Spindown, *Nancy Johnson, 1997. This quilt uses the same primary cell as the quilts on pages 44, 49, 52, 56, and 61 but color, fabric, and symmetry arrangements produce a comparably different design.*

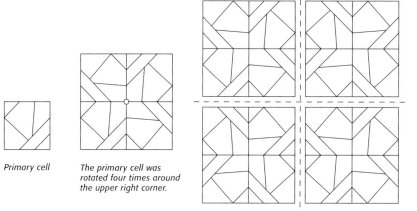

Primary cell

The primary cell was rotated four times around the upper right corner.

The four units were then mirrored to complete the design.

Illustration 3.54 Spindown *is an example of mirrored pinwheel (p4g) symmetry.*

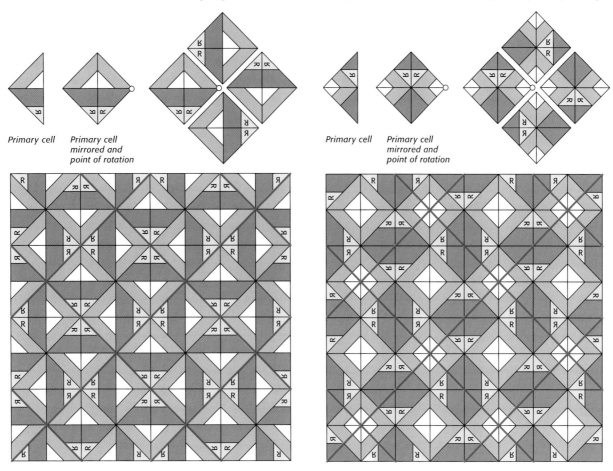

Illustration 3.55. A triangular cell and smaller square tile also produce the same pattern as the square cell and larger tile.

Multiple Patterns from a Single Cell

The same primary cell has been used to illustrate patterns in the first 11 symmetry groups. We have shown 24 patterns generated from that single cell. If diagonally glided patterns are included (see page 21) at least four more patterns can be created. By coloring the cell in different ways you could get even more pattern possibilities.

The reference chart on pages 100 through 103 in Chapter 6 summarizes all of the symmetry groups, and you will be able to see patterns generated by the groups side by side, so that the differences between the patterns will be more apparent.

Suzi's Box, *Jinny Beyer, 1975.*
The overall design of this quilt is double mirror (pmm) symmetry and both the patchwork and fabric borders are examples of double mirror (mm) linear symmetry. But the large central hexagonal medallion and the small hexagonal stars are examples of kaleidoscope (p6m) symmetry. The quilt is made of hand block-printed Indian fabrics.

CHAPTER 4

Designing with Two-Dimensional Symmetries:
The Last Six Symmetry Groups

THE FIRST 11 SYMMETRY GROUPS can be illustrated using a square primary cell. The remaining six require a primary cell other than a square. The twelfth symmetry group, for example, requires a right triangle (a square cut in half diagonally). The tile used to create patterns in this symmetry group is a square. The last five require shapes of which multiples will form a diamond or hexagonal tile—a 60° diamond, an equilateral triangle, and a 90°, 60°, 30° triangle. The sixteenth symmetry group has a primary cell that is either a half hexagon, a four-sided kite shape with angles of 120°, 90°, 60°, 90°, or a triangle with angles of 120°, 30°, 30°. The shapes shown in Illustration 4.1 can be used for the layout of patterns in these remaining symmetry groups.

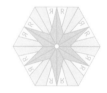

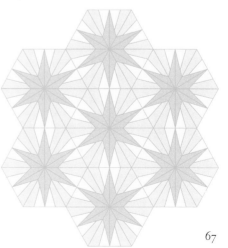

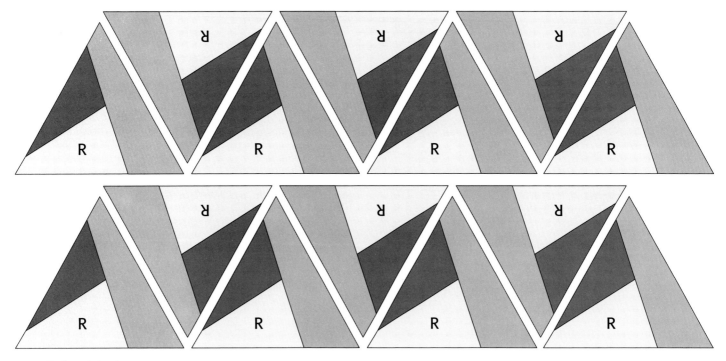

Equilateral triangle

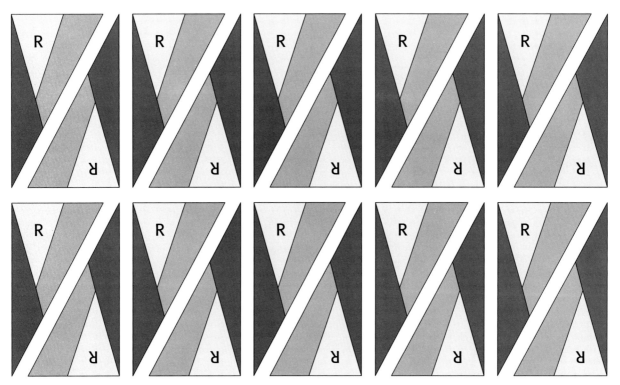

30°, 60°, 90° triangle

Illustration 4.1. Cell page. Photocopy these pages onto plain paper and acetate to use for experimenting with the next six symmetries.

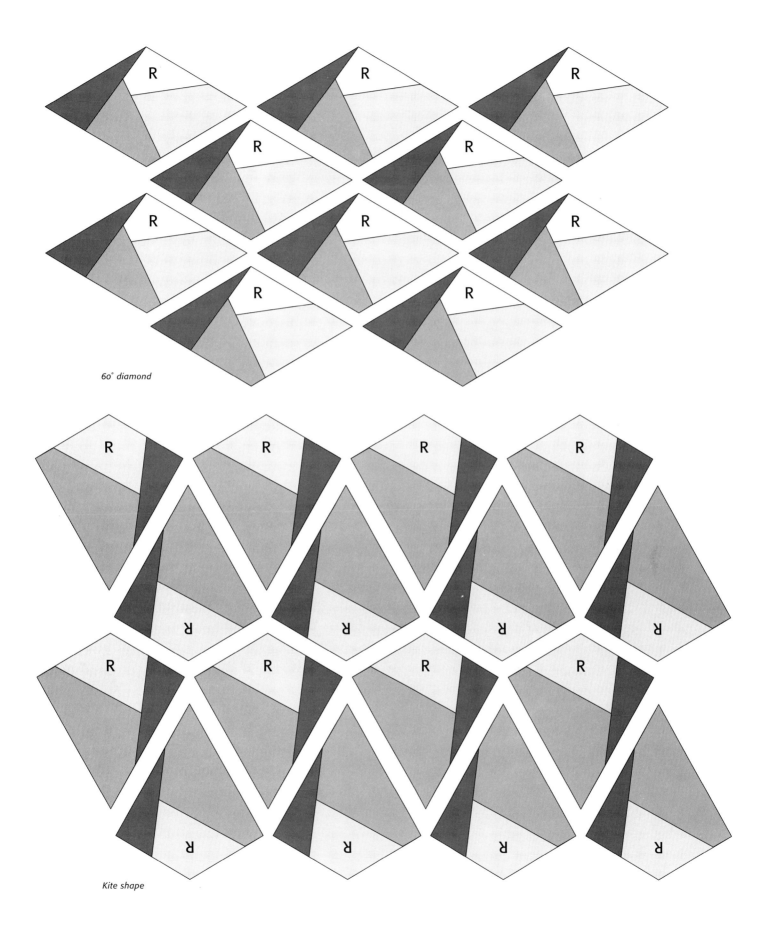

60° diamond

Kite shape

Original cell

   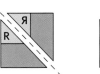

Cut the square cell that was used in the first 11 symmetries in half diagonally. Four different triangular cells occur, depending on how the square is cut.

Mirror the primary cell along the long side.

Rotate four of the resulting squares around one of the new 90° angles.

Illustration 4.2. Creating patterns with traditional block symmetry.

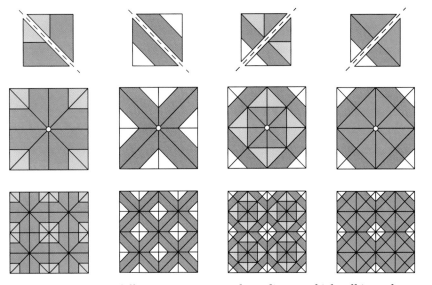

Illustration 4.3. Four different patterns occur depending on which cell is used.

12. Traditional Block (p4m) Symmetry

The traditional block (p4m) symmetry group is one of the most commonly used, particularly in patchwork and quilt design. In fact, the vast majority of all traditional quilt blocks are made up of this symmetry, which is why I gave it this name. The primary cell is a 90°, 45°, 45° (half-square) triangle, and the tile is created by mirroring the long side of the triangle, then rotating four of those units along one of the angles along the mirror line. Eight primary cells are required to create the repeating tile, four of them right side up and four of them mirrored or reversed.

To practice creating patterns in this symmetry group you can cut the square cell from the first 11 symmetries in half diagonally. Working with eight identical acetate triangles, make four sets of mirrored pairs, with the mirror along the long side of the triangle. Stack the pairs on top of each other all oriented in the same direction and then rotate them around one of the two corners formed by the mirror line. The resulting tile can then be repeated to form the overall pattern. Four different patterns occur depending on which cell is used. Where the point of rotation occurs is very important. After the cell is mirrored, it is rotated on one of the two *new* 90° angles, not the original one from the triangle. If the mirrored cells are rotated on the original 90° angle in the triangle, the mirrored pinwheel (p4g) pattern will occur.

The following illustrations show several examples of traditional block (p4m) symmetry pattern.

Standard Notation—p4m

The standard notation system labels this symmetry p4m. Since the *m* immediately follows the 4, the primary cell must first be mirrored (m) and the result is rotated four times (p4) on the right angle, which is formed by the mirror.

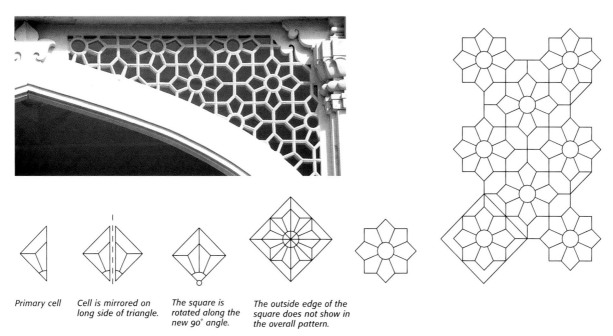

Primary cell   Cell is mirrored on long side of triangle.

The square is rotated along the new 90° angle.

The outside edge of the square does not show in the overall pattern.

Illustration 4.4. *Pattern found in cut stone work above window in Jaipur, India; the pattern is an example of traditional block (p4m) symmetry. The diagrams show how the pattern can be created.*

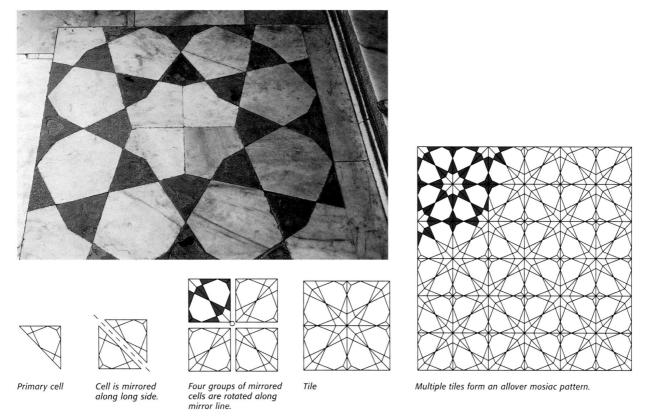

Primary cell   Cell is mirrored along long side.

Four groups of mirrored cells are rotated along mirror line.

Tile

Multiple tiles form an allover mosaic pattern.

Illustration 4.5. *Mosaic floor in Amber Palace in Jaipur, India, showing an example of traditional block (p4m) symmetry.*

Midnight Star, *Robin Morrison, 1998. This quilt is an example of traditional block (p4m) symmetry.*

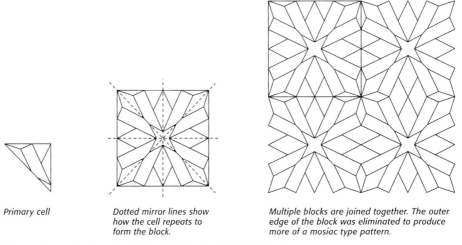

Primary cell

Dotted mirror lines show
how the cell repeats to
form the block.

Multiple blocks are joined together. The outer
edge of the block was eliminated to produce
more of a mosiac type pattern.

Illustration 4.6. Creating Midnight Star *by Robin Morrison.*

Illustration 4.7. Creating patterns with three rotation (p3) symmetry.

13. Three Rotation (p3) Symmetry

A 60° diamond primary cell is required to create the tile for the three-rotation (p3) symmetry group. No mirror or reverse cells are needed. The cell is simply rotated just as was done in the midpoint rotation (p2) and pinwheel (p4) symmetry groups. Photocopy the diamond cells shown in Illustration 4.1, cut three of them out and stack them on top of each other all oriented in the same direction. Place a pin on one of the two 120° angles and rotate the diamonds around that angle until they form a hexagon. This tile is then repeated to form the overall design. It does not matter which of the two angles are rotated. The same pattern will occur in either case.

The patterns shown in Illustrations 4.8 and 4.9 are examples of three rotation (p3) symmetry.

Standard Notation—p3

The p3 designation refers to the primary cell (p) with three (3) rotations required to create the tile.

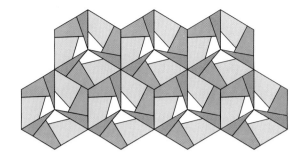

Primary cell   Tile

Illustration 4.8. Detail of Puzzle Panic *by Judy Spahn (page 233) showing three rotation (p3) symmetry.*

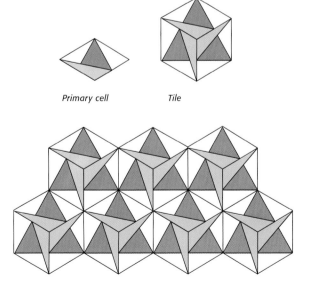

Illustration 4.9. Origami, Jinny Beyer, 1997. An example of three rotation (p3) symmetry.

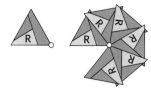

Illustration 4.10. Creating patterns with six rotation (p6) symmetry.

Standard Notation—p6

The p6 label shows that the primary cell (p) requires six rotations (6) to complete the tile.

14. Six Rotation (p6) Symmetry

Patterns in the six-rotation (p6) symmetry group can be produced with either an equilateral triangle or a kite shape. Six cells, all right side up, are needed to create the tile, and the cells are simply rotated around a 60° angle. To create the tile, cut out six of the equilateral triangles shown in Illustration 4.1; stack them on top of each other, oriented in the same direction; put a pin in one of the corners; and rotate them around until they form a hexagon-shaped tile. When an equilateral triangle is used to create this symmetry group, three different patterns can be generated depending on which corner is rotated, as shown in Illustration 4.11.

Illustrations 4.12 and 4.13 show other examples of six rotation (p6) symmetry.

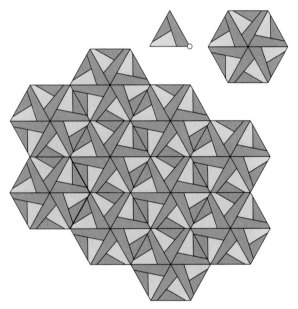

Illustration 4.11. Three different patterns are possible depending on which angle is rotated.

Illustration 4.12. Detail of Rhapsody *by Jinny Beyer (page 166) shows an example of six rotation (p6) symmetry.*

Illustration 4.13. Fabric designs showing examples of six rotation (p6) symmetry.

Primary cell   *Mirror one of the*   *Rotate three of the*   *Tile*
                   sides of the triangle. *resulting diamonds around*
                                           one of the 120° angles.

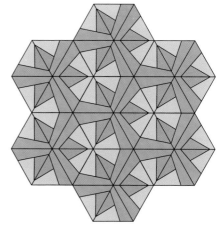

Illustration 4.14. Creating patterns with mirror and three rotation (p3m1) symmetry.

The same pattern will occur no matter which side of the triangle is rotated.

Illustration 4.15. Fabric design showing example.of three-rotation (p3m1) symmetry.

15. Mirror and Three-Rotation (p3m1) Symmetry

An equilateral triangle is also used as the primary cell when creating patterns in the mirror and three-rotation (p3m1) symmetry group, but this time, since a mirror occurs, the triangles will need to be photocopied onto acetate. The pattern for this symmetry group is created by first mirroring one of the sides of the triangle and then rotating the result three times along the angle formed by the mirror. If you put mirrors on all sides of the primary cell, you will see the pattern.

To create the tile, make three identical mirrored pairs of triangles. Stack the resulting diamonds on top of each other oriented in the same direction, and rotate them around one of the 120° angles. No matter which side of the triangle is first mirrored the overall design will remain the same.

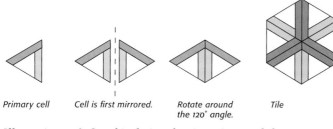

Primary cell   *Cell is first mirrored.*   *Rotate around*   *Tile*
                                                the 120° angle.

Illustration 4.16. Graphic design showing mirror and three-rotation (p3m1) symmetry. Compare this to a similar type design shown on page 78, but with the three rotations and a mirror (p31m) symmetry. Different symmetry operations create subtle differences in the pattern.

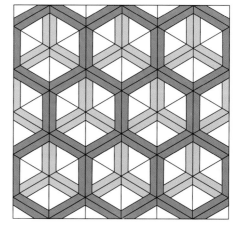

Pattern

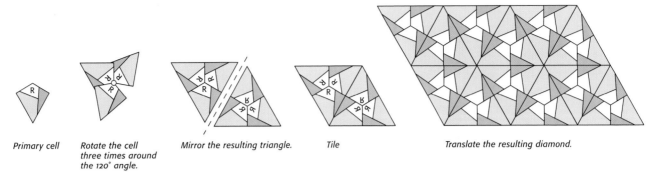

Primary cell   Rotate the cell three times around the 120° angle.   Mirror the resulting triangle.   Tile   Translate the resulting diamond.

Illustration 4.17. *Creating patterns with three rotations and a mirror (p31m) symmetry.*

16. Three Rotations and a Mirror (p31m) Symmetry

The primary cell for patterns in this symmetry group can be either a half hexagon, half of a 60° diamond, or a kite shape (angles in the kite shape are 120°, 90°, 60°, 90°). A total of six primary cells are required to create the tile, three of them right side up and three of them reversed. Using the kite shape from Illustration 4.1 photocopied onto acetate, stack three of the cells right side up on top of each other and all oriented in the same direction. Rotate them around the 120° angle until they form an equilateral triangle. Make another triangle exactly the same, then mirror it to form the diamond-shaped tile. These diamonds then translate to create the pattern. Illustration 4.17 shows the tile created with the kite shape. Illustration 4.19 shows the half diamond that can be used with this symmetry.

Illustrations 4.18, 4.20, and 4.21 show patterns formed with three rotations and a mirror symmetry with diagrams showing the cell and tile.

Illustration 4.18. *Fabric design showing examples of three rotations and a mirror (p31m) symmetry.*

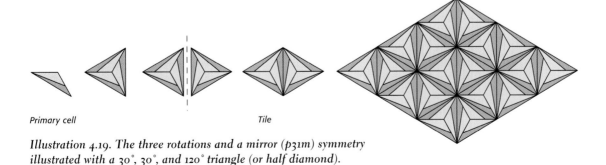

Primary cell   Tile

Illustration 4.19. *The three rotations and a mirror (p31m) symmetry illustrated with a 30°, 30°, and 120° triangle (or half diamond).*

Satsuma Plate, *Yoko Sawanoban, 1977.*

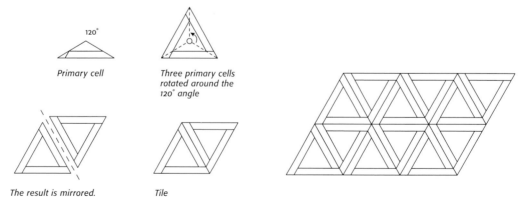

120°

Primary cell

Three primary cells rotated around the 120° angle

The result is mirrored.

Tile

Illustration 4.20. Satsuma Plate is an example of three rotations and a mirror (p31m) symmetry. The diagrams show how the design is created. Compare this to Illustration 4.16, which has a similar appearance, but uses a different symmetry operation which creates subtle differences.

Cupid Misfires, *Kathrynn Kuhn, 1994.*

*Primary cell (½ of a
60° diamond)*   *Three cells
rotated.*

*The rotated cells are mirrored to
produce the tile.*   *Tiles repeat to form the pattern. Shading changes the
appearance of the design.*

Illustration 4.21. Cupid Misfires *is an example of three rotations and a mirror
(p31m) symmetry. The diagrams show how the design is created. See also page 155.*

Standard Notations—p3m1 and p31m

It is very easy to confuse the p3m1 and the p31m labels, yet both of these symmetry groups produce very different patterns. Both have three-fold rotation and both contain mirrors. But if you remember how the standard notation system is organized (see pages 24 through 29), it all makes more sense. My interpretation of the notations is as follows: because three rotations are required in each of these symmetries, there must be a 120° angle around which the rotation takes place.

With p3m1, the *m* comes immediately after the 3, which means that the primary cell must be mirrored first and then rotated three times (p3). Therefore, you must begin with an equilateral triangle which has angles of 60°. After the shape is mirrored, the 60° angle

Exercise 1

Differentiating Between p3m1 and p31m Symmetries

These designs are either p3m1 or p31m symmetry. Can you determine which symmetry operation creates each one? Place a piece of tracing paper over the designs and draw the underlying grid to determine the primary cell. The answers are in Appendix C.

1.

4.

doubles to 120° and the rotation can then take place around one of
the two 120° angles formed by the mirror line.

    With the p31m, the *m* in the fourth position indicates that the
primary cell must first be rotated three times (p3) before it is
mirrored *m*. The *1* is used in these labels to make clear the position
of the (m). The *1* is basically a separator meaning that no action
takes along one of the other sides of the cell. Because the rotation
takes place first in this symmetry the original cell must have a 120°
angle around which the rotation can occur. A kite shape, half
hexagon, and half of a 60° diamond will all work for this symmetry.

    The exercise below should help you better understand the
difference between p31m and p3m1.

2.

3.

5.

6.

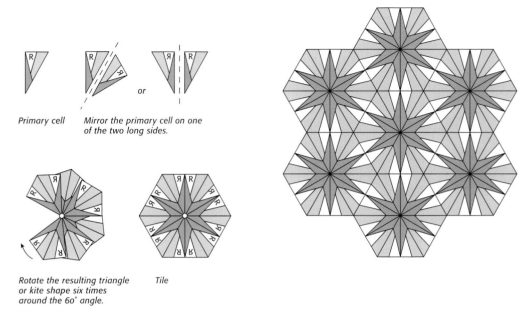

Illustration 4.22. Creating patterns with kaleidoscope (p6m) symmetry.

17. Kaleidoscope (p6m) Symmetry

When looking through a kaleidoscope one sees mirrors on all sides of a shape, producing intricately changing patterns. Different designs occur depending on the angle of the mirrors inside the kaleidoscope. While several of the previously discussed symmetry groups can be formed by putting mirrors on all sides of the primary cell, this one looked to me more like a true kaleidoscope, which is why I have given it the name.

Patterns in the kaleidoscope (p6m) symmetry group are is formed almost exactly the same way as those in the mirror and three-rotation (p3m1) symmetry group. This time, however, a different shaped triangle (90°, 60°, 30°) is the primary cell. The pattern can be seen by placing mirrors on all sides of the triangle. To create the tile, make six mirrored pairs of triangles. Mirror either of the two longest sides, as the same pattern will be produced in either case. If the longest side is mirrored, the result will be a kite shape; if the next-longest side is mirrored, the result will be an equilateral triangle. Stack the mirrored pairs on top of each other, all oriented in the same direction, and rotate them six times to form the tile. In the case of the kite shape, be sure the rotation occurs around the 60° angle (Illustration 4.22).

Standard Notation—p6m

The labeling system for p6m is as follows: because there is an *m* immediately after the six, the primary cell must first be mirrored (m) before it is rotated six times (p6).

Primary cell

Tile

Illustration 4.23. A diamond-shaped tile can also be created by mirroring the long side of the cell, rotating the resulting 120° angle and mirroring that triangle. Either way the same pattern results.

A diamond-shaped tile can be used to form the pattern, as shown in Illustration 4.23, but creating the tile is a little more involved. Since the overall pattern is the same, I find it easiest just to create the hexagonally shaped tile.

The detail of *Suzi's Box*, shown here, and the two examples on the following page show other examples of kaleidoscope (p6m) symmetry.

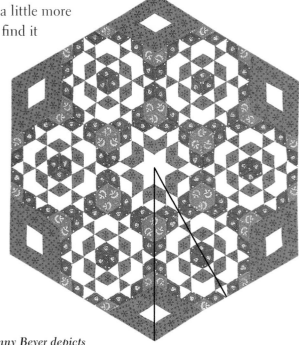

Illustration 4.24. Detail from Suzi's Box (page 66) by Jinny Beyer depicts kaleidoscope (p6m) symmetry. Each hexagonal star has p6m symmetry as well as the larger hexagon containing seven of the smaller hexagons.

Christmas Kaleidoscope, *Nancy Johnson, 1997.* **This quilt is an example of kaleidoscope (p6m) symmetry.**

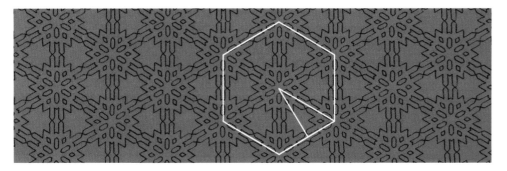

Illustration 4.25. *Fabric design showing example of kaleidoscope (p6m) symmetery.*

Summary of Two-Dimensional Symmetry Groups

This chapter and the last have explained in detail how, by using the 17 symmetry groups, a vast array of two-dimensional patterns can be created. A thorough understanding of these concepts will help immensely as you work to create your own patterns, and it is especially important for understanding how interlocking or tessellating designs are developed. The best way to learn is by manipulating the primary cells yourself. I urge you to reread these two chapters, work with the primary cells provided, and lay out patterns in each of the symmetry groups, using the cell sheets on page 32 and pages 68 and 69.

Armed with this experience, you will see the wonderful opportunities for design that are presented in Chapters 6 through 11. Pages 100 through 103 of Chapter 6 have a quick reference chart that summarizes how patterns in all of the symmetry groups are created. Seeing the possibilities side by side in this chart will aid in further understanding of the symmetry groups.

Ray of Light, *Jinny Beyer, 1977.*
The overall quilt is an example of double mirror (pmm) symmetry, a two-dimensional symmetry. Three different linear symmetries can be found in the border patterns: double mirror (mm), vertical mirror (m1), and translation (11).

CHAPTER 5

Designing with *Linear Symmetry Groups*

EXAMPLES OF PATTERNS created by using the linear symmetry groups can be found in all forms of decorative art. In artifacts and structures that have derived from the most ancient times, one can see linear patterns adorning crockery, jewelry, tapestries, carpets, tombs, walls, windows, and buildings. Today, walk down the street of any city and look at doorways, windows, sidewalks, and walls, and you will see that linear patterns abound. Linear patterns can form exciting borders for any type of surface design, and understanding how to create the patterns is easy.

Standard Notations

The standard notation for labeling the linear symmetry groups is similar to that for the two-dimensional symmetry groups, but in this notation there is no symbol for the cell. The label for each symmetry group consists of two symbols, which are an indication that no more than two operations can be done to a cell to generate a linear symmetry. Sometimes only one operation is done, and if so, there is a *1* indicating no change. Just as in the two-dimensional symmetries, *m* stands for mirror, *g* stands for glide, and *2* indicates a 180° rotation. If there is an *m* in the first position it means that there is a vertical mirror in the symmetry. An *m* in the second position indicates that there is a horizontal mirror in the symmetry.

The Seven Linear Symmetry Groups

Once you have an understanding of the 17 two-dimensional symmetry groups and how to lay them out, the linear ones are not at all difficult. There are only seven of them, and they follow exactly the same movements—translation, rotation, glide, and mirror. Therefore, this chapter will not go into detailed instructions on the specific movements required to lay out the symmetries. If you become confused refer back to the corresponding section in Chapter 3.

Primary Cell

The same cell that illustrated the first 11 symmetry groups has also been used for the linear symmetry patterns. Once again, a tile is first created from one or more primary cells and that tile repeats to form the pattern. But now instead of completely filling the surface, the tile only repeats in a single direction.

In the 17 two-dimensional symmetry groups more than one pattern often can be created from a given symmetry, depending on which side of the cell is rotated, mirrored, etc. The same is true with the linear groups. Though there are only seven linear symmetry groups, I have found 24 different patterns that can be created from a single square cell.

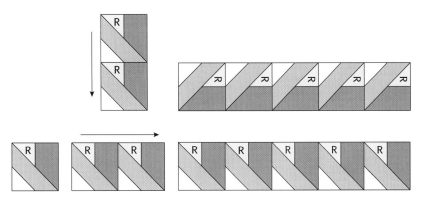

Translate the cell horizontally or vertically.

Illustration 5.1. Creating patterns with translation (11) linear symmetry.

The Linear Symmetry Groups

1. Translation (11) Linear Symmetry

In translation linear symmetry, the primary cell is the tile and that single tile will create two different patterns. One pattern occurs when the cell is translated horizontally and another pattern when the cell is translated vertically as illustrated. (See translation (p1) symmetry on page 34.)

Illustrations 5.2 through 5.4 are also examples of translation linear symmetry.

Illustration 5.2. Fabric design showing example of translation (11) linear symmetry.

Illustration 5.3. Graphic design showing example of translation (11) linear symmetry.

Illustration 5.4. Detail of Ray of Light *by Jinny Beyer (page 86) shows a border with translation (11) linear symmetry.*

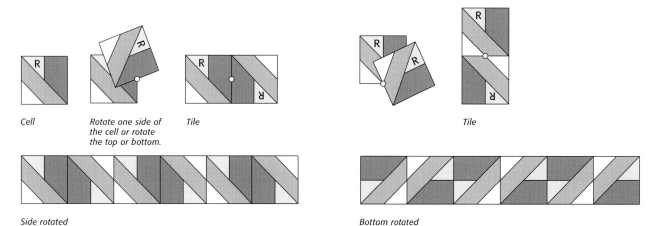

Cell

Rotate one side of the cell or rotate the top or bottom.

Tile

Tile

Side rotated

Bottom rotated

Illustration 5.5. Midpoint rotation or half-turn linear (12) symmetry.

2. Midpoint Rotation or Half-Turn (12) Linear Symmetry

Two different linear patterns occur in the midpoint rotation symmetry group, depending on whether one of the sides of the cell is rotated or the top or bottom is rotated as shown in Illustration 5.5. Two cells make up the tile, one cell rotated 180° from the other. (See midpoint or half-turn rotation (p2) symmetry on page 36).

Illustrations 5.6 through 5.8 show midpoint rotation (12) linear symmetry.

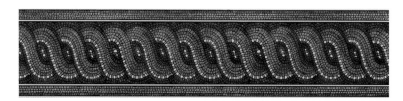

Illustration 5.6. Graphic design showing example of midpoint rotation (12) linear symmetry.

Illustrations 5.7. Detail of border found in inlay design at Fakepursikri, India, showing an example of midpoint rotation (12) linear symmetry.

Illustration 5.8. Graphic design showing example of midpoint rotation (12) linear symmetry.

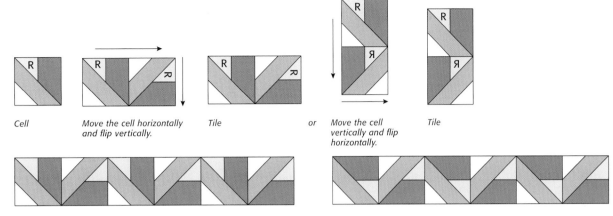

Illustration 5.9. Glide (1g) linear symmetry.

3. Glide (1g) Linear Symmetry

With the glide (lg) linear symmetry group, the primary cell is glided horizontally, vertically or diagonally. Four patterns result depending on how the glide occurs.

Two patterns occur when the glide takes place on one of the two sides of the cell or the top or bottom, as shown in the illustrations above. Two additional patterns (not shown here) occur when the cell is diagonally glided. (See p. 21.) See glide (pg) symmetry on page 42.

Illustration 5.10 shows examples of glide linear symmetry.

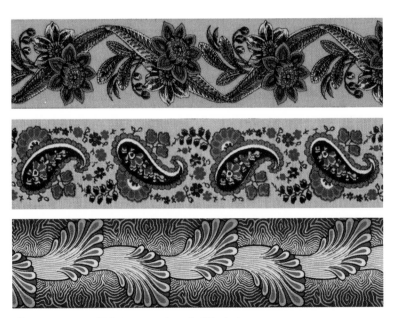

Illustration 5.10. Fabric examples of glide (1g) symmetry.

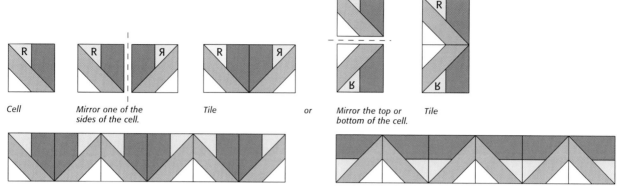

Illustration 5.11. Vertical mirror (m1) linear symmetry.

4. Vertical Mirror (m1) Linear Symmetry

In the vertical mirror (m1) symmetry group two cells make up the tile. Those two cells are mirrored on one of the four edges, generating two pattern possibilities—one when one of the sides is mirrored and the other when the top or bottom is mirrored. The mirrored tiles continue single file to produce the pattern. (See mirror (pm) symmetry on page 47.)

Illustrations 5.12 and 5.13 show additional examples of vertical mirror (m1) linear symmetry.

Illustration 5.12. Border detail on the edge of a balcony in Jaipur, India, shows vertical mirror (m1) linear symmetry.

Illustration 5.13. Fabric designs showing examples of vertical mirror (m1) linear symmetry.

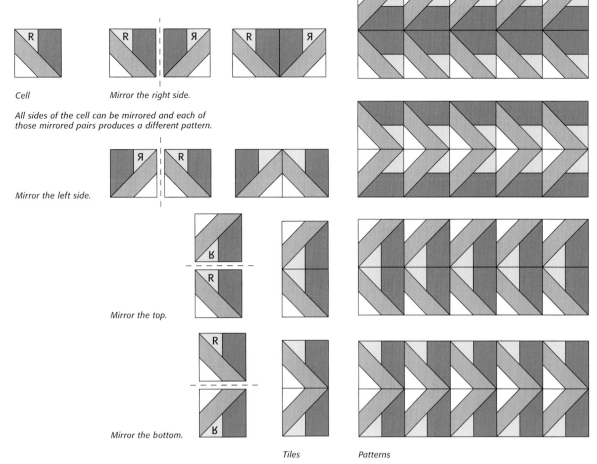

Cell

Mirror the right side.

All sides of the cell can be mirrored and each of those mirrored pairs produces a different pattern.

Mirror the left side.

Mirror the top.

Mirror the bottom.

Tiles   Patterns

Illustration 5.14. Horizontal mirror (1m) linear symmetry.

5. Horizontal Mirror (1m) Linear Symmetry

Two cells also make up the tile for patterns in the horizontal mirror (1m) linear symmetry group. But this time instead of putting the tiles end to end lengthwise, turn them and put them together sideways. The pattern is therefore two cells wide instead of one.

Because of the way the tile is turned to form the pattern, four different designs can be created with this symmetry. Each side of the cell can be mirrored, and each set of mirrored pairs will produce a different pattern.

The quilt *Flying Geese* and Illustration 5.15 show examples of horizontal mirror (1m) linear symmetry.

Illustration 5.15. Fabric design containing two different horizontal mirror (1m) linear symmetry borders.

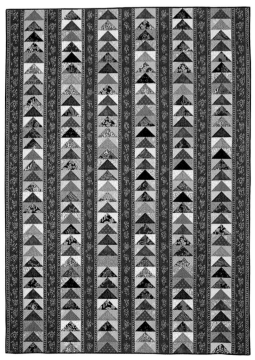

Flying Geese, *Nancy Johnson, 1985. This traditional quilt is an example of horizontal mirror (1m) linear symmetry.*

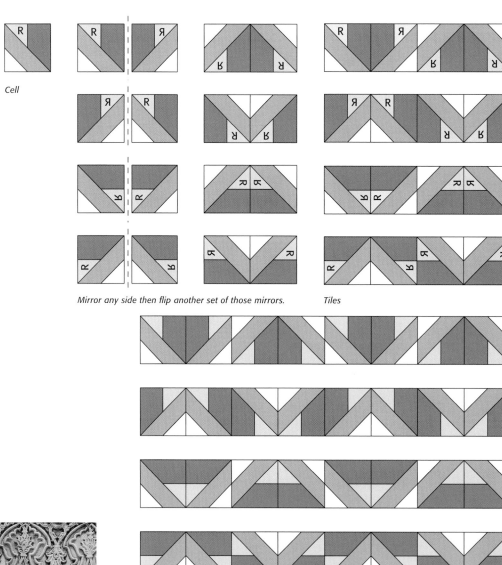

Cell

Mirror any side then flip another set of those mirrors.   *Tiles*

Patterns

Illustration 5.16. Glided mirror (mg) linear symmetry.

Illustration 5.17. The stonework in Fakepursikm, India, is an example of a pattern generated with the glided mirror (mg) linear symmetry.

Illustration 5.18. Fabric designs showing examples of glided mirror (mg) linear symmetry.

6. Glided Mirror (mg) Linear Symmetry

Four cells make up the tile for patterns in the glided mirror (mg) linear symmetry group. To create the tile using this symmetry, two cells are mirrored and then another set of identical mirrored cells are moved horizontally and flipped vertically. Just as in horizontal mirror symmetry, all four sides of the cell can be mirrored to produce four completely different patterns. (See glided staggered mirror (pmg) symmetry on page 54.)

Illustrations 5.17 and 5.18 show examples of patterns generated with the glided mirror (mg) linear symmetry.

Primary cell

Four different patterns can be formed depending on which sides of the cell have the mirrors.

Illustration 5.19. Double mirror (mm) linear symmetry.

7. Double Mirror (mm) Linear Symmetry

The last linear symmetry group requires four cells to make the repeating tile. There are both vertical and horizontal mirrors in this symmetry. Two cells are mirrored and then those two are mirrored again. Each side of the cell can be mirrored to produce four different patterns.

Illustrations 5.20 and 5.21 show other examples of double mirror (mm) linear symmetry. (For a reference chart on all of the two-dimensional and linear symmetry groups, refer to pages 100 through 103 of the next chapter.)

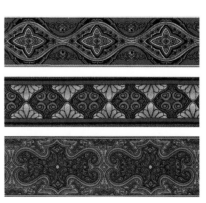

Illustration 5.20. Fabric border designs showing examples of double mirror (mm) linear symmetry.

Turning Corners with Border (Linear) Symmetries

When framing a piece of work with a decorative border, one of the prime considerations is how to turn the corner neatly. When a corner does not flow along with the rest of the design, the appearance of the overall piece is affected. The type of symmetry that the border design has determines how you treat the border in order to turn the corners effectively.

Leave the corner space free to be filled in later. At that time a motif can be added that allows the design to flow smoothly around the corner. The border along one edge must end at the corner at exactly the same place as the border along the adjacent edge. With certain symmetries, this means that the border on one side must be the mirror image of the adjacent border. The entire length of the border cannot be mirror imaged, however, or the other corners will not match. Therefore, I like to reverse the border at the center of the piece being framed. This is a particularly useful technique, regardless of the symmetry involved, when working with a piece that is longer than it is wide. If you match the corners and bring the two borders to the exact center, they will create a mirror image where they meet.

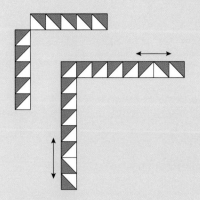

1. Translation (11)
For the corner to turn symmetrically, you must reverse the border at the center of the frame (indicated by the arrows).

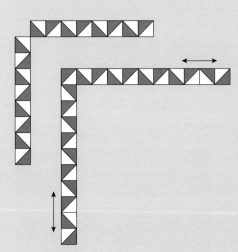

2. Glide (1g)
For the corner to turn symmetrically, you must reverse the border at the center of the frame (indicated by the arrows).

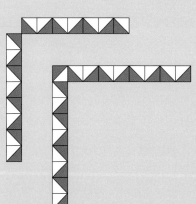

3. Vertical mirror (m1)
This symmetry will automatically turn the corner.

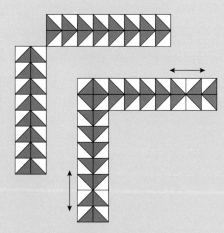

4. Horizontal mirror (1m)
For the corner to turn symmetrically, you must reverse the border at the center of the frame (indicated by the arrows).

The illustrations on these pages show borders done with each of the seven linear symmetry groups. With the translation, midpoint rotation, glide, and vertical mirror symmetry patterns, to turn the corner symmetrically, the border must reverse (mirror) at the center of the piece being framed. Double arrows on the applicable borders indicate the center of the piece and show a mirror image of the border. Vertical mirror, glided mirror, and double mirror symmetry will automatically turn the corner without a reverse of one of the pieces.

With each of the patterns, the first illustration shows two sections of the border without any mirroring of the design. The second illustration shows a reversal of the border (if applicable), and the corner filled in.

In order for corners to turn neatly, you must always end the design at the same place on all sides. Leave the corner blank and then fill it in later with something that will be appropriate with the design.

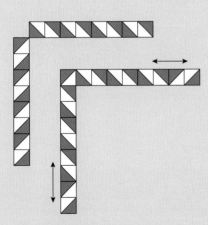

5. Midpoint rotation (12)
For the corner to turn symmetrically, you must reverse the border at the center of the frame (indicated by the arrows).

6. Glided mirror (mg)
This symmetry will automatically turn the corner.

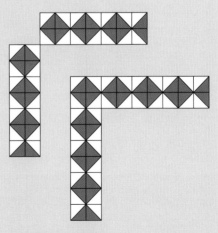

7. Double mirror (mm)
This symmetry will automatically turn the corner.

Inner City, *Jinny Beyer, 1978.*
The tessellating pattern of this quilt is an example of three rotations and a mirror (p31m) symmetry.

CHAPTER 6

Experimenting with Symmetry

NOW THAT YOU HAVE STUDIED the two-dimensional and linear symmetry groups, you are ready to experiment with many of the dynamic design options that present themselves from an understanding of symmetry. Sections of this chapter are structured like a workbook with exercises and ideas on how to make symmetry work for you no matter what your area of design. Work through the exercises. Then, where applicable, refer to the answers in the Appendix. The quick reference charts on the following pages summarize the 17 two-dimensional and 7 linear symmetry groups. They will help you with the exercises and enable you to see at a glance many of the patterns that can be generated simply by manipulating the cells.

The 17 Symmetry Groups

Primary cell: an asymmetrical unit—the smallest portion of the pattern that can be repeated
Tile: the smallest number of primary cells that fit together to form a repeating translation unit or tile

Symmetry	Primary Cell	Transformation	Tile	Pattern
1. Translation (p1) The primary cell is the tile and is translated.				
2. Midpoint or Half-Turn Rotation (p2) The primary cell (p) is rotated 180° (2) at the midpoint of a side. It can look different depending on whether it is rotated from one of the sides, the top or bottom, or both the top and the bottom. The three tile possibilities are shown.		*Variation 1, rotated from the side*		
		Variation 2, rotated from the top or bottom		
		Variation 3, rotated from all sides		
3. Pinwheel or Quarter-Turn (p4) Rotation The primary cell (p) is rotated four times (4) around one of the corners. This symmetry produces the pinwheel block. Two different patterns can result depending on whether it is rotated from the upper left or lower right corner or from the upper right or lower left corners.		*Variation 1, rotated from lower right and upper left*		
		Variation 2, rotated from upper right and lower left		
4. Glide (pg) The primary cell (p) is glided (g). To glide, the cell is either moved horizontally and flipped vertically (variation 1) or moved vertically and flipped horizontally (variation 2). Two additional patterns (not shown here) can be created with diagonal glides to the primary cell.		*Variation 1, move horizontally, flip vertically*		
		Variation 2, move vertically, flip horizontally		
5. Double Glide (pgg) The primary cell (p) is glided both horizontally and vertically (gg) to create the tile. Two additional patterns (not shown here) can be created with diagonal glides to the primary cell.				
6. Mirror (pm) The primary cell (p) is mirrored (m) to form the tile. The result looks different depending on whether the sides are mirrored or the top and bottom. Both tile possibilities are shown.		*Variation 1, sides mirrored*		
		Variation 2, top and bottom mirrored		
7. Staggered Mirror (cm) The primary cell is mirrored (m), then mirrored pairs are staggered, or centered (c), to form the tile. A jagged tile is difficult to work with so the tile is squared off by moving the one piece to fill the hole. Just as in mirror symmetry above, the result is different depending on which side of the tile is mirrored. A smaller, triangular primary cell can also be used. That is then mirrored to form the tile. That cell is outlined in red.		*Variation 1, sides mirrored*	*Stagger*	
		Variation 2, top and bottom mirrored	*Stagger*	

Symmetry	Primary Cell	Transformation	Tile	Pattern

8. Glided Staggered Mirror (pmg) The primary cell (p) is mirrored (m), and the pairs are staggered as in staggered mirror symmetry, but this time, one of the sets is glided (g). If the mirrored pairs are staggered horizontally, then one pair is flipped vertically (variation 1). If the mirrored pairs are staggered vertically, then one pair is flipped horizontally (variation 2). The tile is squared off by moving the one cell to fill the hole.

Variation 1, stagger and flip vertically

Variation 2, stagger and flip horizontally

9. Double Mirror (pmm) The primary cell (p) is mirrored vertically, then both of those are mirrored horizontally (mm). This is the same as putting mirrors on all sides of the primary cell.

10. Staggered Double Mirror (cmm) The primary cell is mirrored twice, as in the double mirror (mm) symmetry above, and these mirrored cells are staggered, or centered (c). A smaller triangular cell can also be used; that cell is double mirrored to form the tile. The triangular cell is indicated in red.

Two different patterns can be made with this symmetry, depending on which side is mirrored first.

Variation 1   Variation 2

Variation 3   Variation 4

11. Mirrored Pinwheel (p4g) The pinwheel (p4) is glided (g), which produces the same effect as if it was mirrored on all sides to produce this symmetry. It takes four mirrored units to create the repeating tile. The pattern can look very different depending on which corner of the primary cell is rotated. The pattern can also be generated from a triangular cell (outlined in red), which is rotated four times and then mirrored on the long side.

Variation 1, rotated from lower right

Variation 2, rotated from upper right

Variation 3, rotated from upper left

Variation 4, rotated from lower left

12. Traditional Block (p4m) The primary cell (p) is a right-angle triangle that is mirrored (m), then that unit is rotated four times along the angle created by this mirror (4). The triangular cell used is the same as the one in the triangle version of staggered mirror symmetry.

The 17 Symmetry Groups *continued*

Symmetry	Primary Cell	Transformation	Tile	Pattern

13. Three Rotation (p3) The primary cell (p) is rotated three times (3) on one of the 120° angles.

14. Six Rotation (p6) The primary cell (p) is rotated six times (6). The effect can be very different depending on which one of the three corners is rotated. The dot on the primary cell shows which corner was rotated for each tile.

15. Mirror and Three Rotations (p3m1) The primary cell (p) is first mirrored (m), and then the resulting diamond is rotated three times (3) at one of the 120° angles. In essence you are putting mirrors on all sides of the shape.

Primary cell mirrored

Three mirrored units rotated

16. Three Rotations and a Mirror (p31m) The primary cell (p) is first rotated three times at the 120° angle (3), then the resulting triangle is mirrored (m).

Primary cell rotated three times around the 120° angle

Three rotations mirrored

17. Kaleidoscope (p6m) Either of the two long sides of the primary cell (p) is mirrored (m), the resulting shape is rotated six times (6). In essence you are putting mirrors on all sides of the shape.

Primary cell mirrored along one of the long sides; rotate six of these.

Linear Symmetries

Symmetry	Primary Cell	Tile	Pattern

1. Translation (11) The primary cell is the tile. Two patterns are possible depending on how the tile is turned.

2. Midpoint Rotation (12) The primary cell is rotated at the midpoint of a side. Two patterns occur depending on where the rotation occurs.

3. Glide (1g) The primary cell is glided—either moved horizontally and flipped vertically or moved vertically and flipped horizontally. Two patterns result depending on how the glide occurs.

4. Vertical Mirror (m1) The primary cell is mirrored along a vertical mirror line. For the second pattern it is turned and then mirrored vertically.

5. Horizontal Mirror (1m) The primary cell is mirrored along a horizontal mirror line. Four patterns occur as the cell is turned.

6. Glided Mirror (mg) The primary cell is mirrored, and then alternate mirrored pairs are flipped upside down. Four patterns result depending on which side is mirrored.

7. Double Mirror (mm) The primary cell is mirrored on two sides. Four patterns occur, depending on which sides are mirrored.

Preparing to Experiment

If you own a computer and have a graphics program, the quickest way to experiment is to create the individual cells on your computer, then duplicate, flip, rotate, mirror, etc. It is much faster than photocopying, cutting, and pasting pieces of cards or paper, and it gives you time to try many more possibilities. There are also software programs that have been created specifically for design manipulation. Two such programs, developed by Kevin Lee, were designed primarily for teaching junior-high and high-school math students about symmetry and tessellations. These programs, Tessellmania! and Kaleidomania!, are particularly valuable for anyone wanting to create designs quickly and to learn more about design manipulation.

Tessellmania! is published by The Learning Company, 800-685-6322. Kaleidomania! is published by Key Curriculum Press, 800-995-MATH.

Applying Other Symmetries to the Primary Cell

Once you understand the various symmetry groups, it is possible to look at any design, find the primary cell, and apply other symmetries to the cell. This allows many different pattern options from an already existing design. Some shapes offer more options than others.

Square Primary Cell

A square primary cell offers more design options than any other shape. In fact, as you have seen earlier in this book, if you take a single square primary cell and apply all of the symmetry operations that can be done to a square, there are at least 28 different pattern possibilities. But there are hundreds more patterns that can be created from a single square cell.

Escher's Potato Game

M. C. Escher, experimenting extensively with symmetry, developed his "layman's theory" on filling a surface and worked to discover how many patterns were possible from a single square cell. He used a tile made up of four of the asymmetrical square cells (a 2 × 2 tile) and experimented with how many different ways the four cells could be placed within that tile. He occasionally entertained his children with the "potato game."[1] An asymmetrical image was carved out of a potato and Escher would have his children try to figure out how many different patterns they could create by dipping the potato in ink and stamping it in different ways upon a paper. The rules were that they must use a 2 × 2 tile, in other words, four cells made up the "tile." Because it was not possible to make a mirror image with a single potato, only rota-

---

[1] For a complete explanation of Escher's study of combining cells to create different patterns, see Doris Schattschneider, "Escher's Combinatorial Patterns," *The Electronic Journal of Combinatorics*, vol. 4 (no. 2) 1997, R#17, 31 pages.

1. Tetra

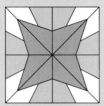

2. Geode

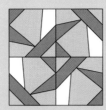

3. Discovery

4. Lone Pine

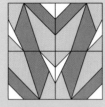

5. Arrowhead

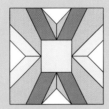

6. Desert Sun

7. Origami

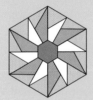

8. Spinning Sunflower

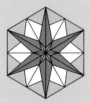

9. Fractured Star

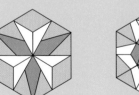

10. Triage

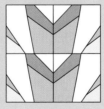

11. Spider Web

12. Angelica

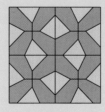

13. Lattice Work

14. Infinity

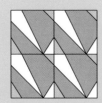

15. Fantail

16. Strata

17. Paper Lantern

Exercise 2

Finding the Primary Cell

Each of the designs on this page is a tile that can be repeated again and again by translation to generate a pattern. All 17 of the two-dimensional symmetry groups are represented. Study each of the tiles and do the following:

1. Find the primary cell.

2. Determine how many primary cells make up the tile.

3. Determine which symmetry operation was used to create the tile.

The answers can be found in Appendix C.

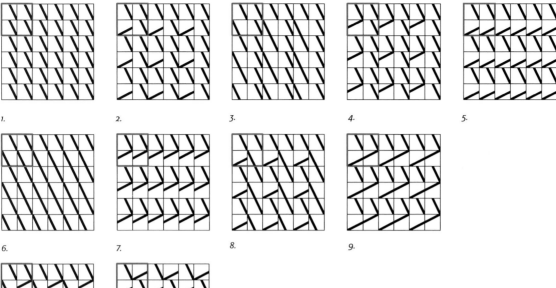

Illustration 6.1. The 23 patterns Escher created working with a tile composed of four cells (two across and two down). He allowed only rotations and translations, no mirror images. The 2 × 2 tile is outlined in red. Illustrations from Doris Schattschneider, "Escher's Combinatorial Patterns," The Electronic Journal of Combinatorics, *vol. 4 (no. 2) 1997, R#17, 31 pages.*

tions could be done. The image could be stamped two up and two down, or all four rotated pinwheel fashion, three up and one turned, etc. Once the 2 × 2 tiles were created, those tiles were then translated over and over to repeat the pattern.

Escher soon discovered that some 2 × 2 tiles produced the same pattern. For instance, as we discussed earlier, if you take a single cell and rotate each of the four corners, four different tiles will result, but when repeating these four tiles over and over by translation, two of those tiles will create the same overall pattern.

When all is said and done, when working with a single cell, arranging that cell in 2 × 2 tiles, and only allowing rotations and translations, there are a total of 23 different patterns that result.

Once Escher had his 2 × 2 tiles, he merely chose to translate them over and over to create the patterns in Illustration 6.1, but my question is why stop at translation? How many more patterns could be developed if the other symmetries are applied to those 2 × 2 tiles as well? It was shown in Chapter 3 that at least 28 different patterns result from the 11 symmetries motions that can be applied to a square cell. So theoretically you could arrive at at least 28 different patterns for each of Escher's 23 2 × 2 tiles for 644 or more patterns.

But wait, five of Escher's 23 tiles have symmetry within the tile—patterns 6 (pm), 12 (pm), 16 (pm), 20 (p4), and 23 (p4). If there is already symmetry within the tile, fewer different patterns are possible when applying other symmetries motions to

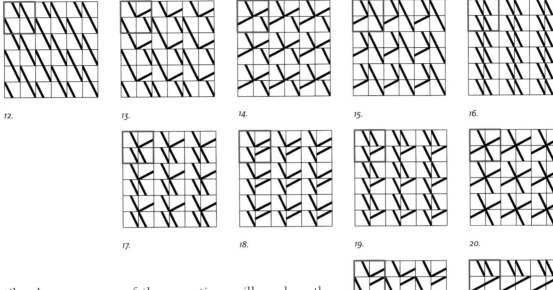

12.   13.   14.   15.   16.

17.   18.   19.   20.

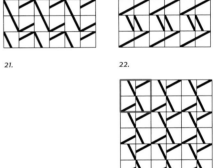

21.   22.

23.

those tiles, because some of the operations will produce the same pattern. With each of the two tiles that have the pm symmetry in one direction only (6 and 16), a total of eight different patterns are possible; with each of the two pinwheel (p4) tiles, only five patterns are possible; with pattern 12, which has mirror (pm) symmetry on two sides, 19 patterns are possible. Since there is no symmetry within the 18 remaining tiles, 24 different patterns (not including those created by diagonal glides) can be created for each of them.

Therefore, working with Escher's criteria of creating 2 × 2 tiles and only allowing rotations and translations within those tiles, if all of the possible symmetries are applied to those tiles, 477 different patterns are possible.

Now what happens if you also allow mirror images within the 2 × 2 tiles? Escher experimented with this as well by carving two stamps instead of one. One of the stamps was the mirror image of the other. This increases the design possibilities immensely. In fact, working with the same 2 × 2 tiles, but allowing for mirror images of some of the cells within the tile and then translating that tile to create a pattern, there are 134 additional pattern possibilities for a total of 157 different designs. Once again these patterns were created by merely translating the 2 × 2 tile, but if other symmetry groups are applied to that tile, as explained above, there are more than 3,000 different patterns that can occur. Not all of those patterns will necessarily be pleasing, but you never know which one will look good until you try it.

Exercise 3

Applying Various Symmetries to the Primary Cell

1. Select one of the designs shown in Exercise 2. Find the primary cell and duplicate it several times onto clear acetate or photocopy the cell and a reverse cell onto paper. (Alternately, re-create the cell on a computer using a graphics program.)

2. If you have chosen a square primary cell create at least 20 different patterns. If you have chosen a right triangle, diamond, or equilateral triangle, create at least seven different patterns. If you have chosen the 30°, 60°, 90° triangle, make six patterns; and if your cell is the kite shape, make four different patterns.

Working with a Square Cell from an Existing Design

The square primary cell has been isolated in the *Tetra* design shown in Illustration 6.2, and you can see that four rotated primary cells make up the 2 × 2 tile that produces the original pattern. This design is an example of pinwheel (p4) symmetry.

Now look at what happens in Illustration 6.3 and see the 24 different patterns that can be produced by applying other symmetries to the primary cell found in the *Tetra* design. Imagine how many more variations could be made by simply changing the color and shading of the cell in different ways. Hundreds more patterns could occur if you work with different 2 × 2 tiles and apply all of the symmetries discussed previously in the example of Escher's experiments.

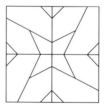

Primary cell   Tetra, *designed by Jinny Beyer*

Illustration 6.2. An example of pinwheel (p4) symmetry.

Translation (p1)

Midpoint rotation (p2) from right side

Midpoint rotation (p2) from bottom

Midpoint rotation (p2) from all sides

Original pattern, pinwheel (p4) from bottom right corner of cell

Pinwheel (p4) from bottom left corner of cell

Glide (pg) from right side of cell

Glide (pg) from bottom of cell

Double glide (pgg)

Mirror (pm) from right side of cell

Mirror (pm) from bottom of cell

Staggered mirror (cm) with mirror at side of cell

Staggered mirror (cm) with mirror at bottom of cell

Staggered double mirror (cmm) with mirror

Glided staggered mirror (pmg) with mirror at side of cell

Glided staggered mirror (pmg) with mirror at bottom of cell

Double mirror (pmm)

Staggered double mirror (cmm) with mirror on right side

Staggered double mirror (cmm)

Staggered double mirror (cmm) with mirror on left side

Mirrored pinwheel (p4gm) with rotation on bottom right corner

Mirrored pinwheel (p4gm) with rotation on bottom left corner

Mirrored pinwheel (p4gm) with rotation on upper left corner

Mirrored pinwheel (p4gm) with rotation on upper right corner

Illustration 6.3. Twenty-four of the patterns that can be created from applying 11 symmetry operations to the Tetra primary cell. Four additional pg and pgg patterns can be created from diagonally gliding the primary cell.

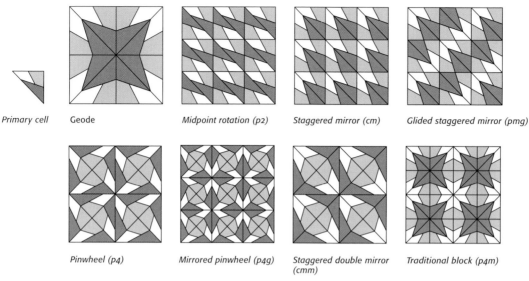

Primary cell   Geode   Midpoint rotation (p2)   Staggered mirror (cm)   Glided staggered mirror (pmg)

Pinwheel (p4)   Mirrored pinwheel (p4g)   Staggered double mirror (cmm)   Traditional block (p4m)

Illustration 6.4. Seven patterns created from the Geode *cell.*

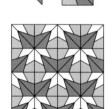

1. Cell midpoint rotated with some additional symmetries applied. Pinwheel (p4), mirrored pinwheel (p4g), and mirror (pm).

2. Cell mirrored with some additional symmetries applied. Staggered mirror, (cm), glided staggered mirror (pmg), and double glide (pgg).

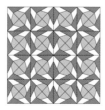

3. Cell rotated around the 90° corner with some additional symmetries applied. Glide (pg) and pinwheel (p4).

Illustration 6.5. *With the right triangle, a square tile can be created in three different ways.*

Working with a Right Triangle Primary Cell

If the cell is a right triangle (90°, 45°, 45°), operations that create patterns in six of the symmetries can be applied, resulting in at least six different patterns. The symmetry groups are midpoint rotation (p2), staggered mirror (cm), glided staggered mirror (pmg), traditional block (p4m), mirrored pinwheel (p4g), and staggered double mirror (cmm). The triangular primary cell from *Geode* is shown in Illustration 6.4 along with diagrams of the seven different patterns that can be created from that cell.

Once again additional patterns can be created by expanding on the primary cell. For instance with the right triangle, a square tile can be created in three different ways. The triangle can be mirrored, it can be midpoint rotated along the long side, or it can be rotated four times around the 90° angle. Once there is a square, then the various symmetries can be applied to create even more patterns. Because there is already a symmetry within the square tile, there are fewer pattern possibilities than if the tile were asymmetrical. A few of the additional designs that can be created with this cell are shown in Illustration 6.5.

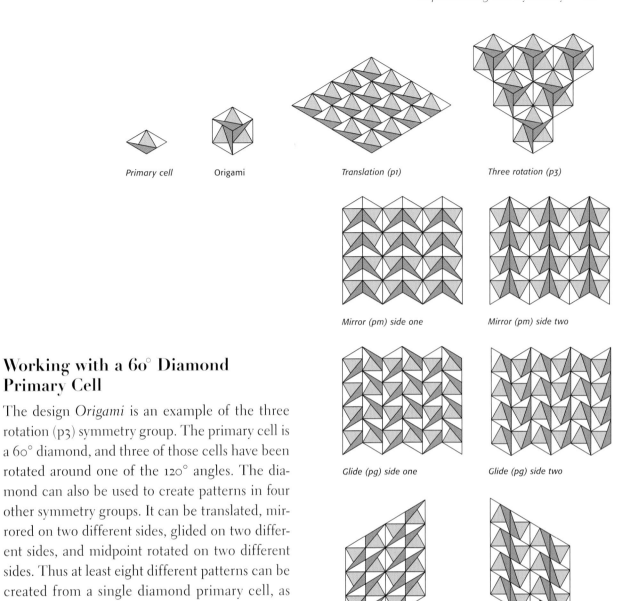

Illustrations 6.6. Eight patterns created from a single diamond primary cell.

Working with a 60° Diamond Primary Cell

The design *Origami* is an example of the three rotation (p3) symmetry group. The primary cell is a 60° diamond, and three of those cells have been rotated around one of the 120° angles. The diamond can also be used to create patterns in four other symmetry groups. It can be translated, mirrored on two different sides, glided on two different sides, and midpoint rotated on two different sides. Thus at least eight different patterns can be created from a single diamond primary cell, as shown in Illustration 6.6.

More patterns could also be developed with this diamond cell by expanding the diamond tile. Instead of a single diamond, you can make a larger diamond composed of four of the smaller ones. The four smaller diamonds can be arranged in a variety of ways, just as the square cells in Escher's potato game were. Then each larger new diamond tile can be arranged in eight different patterns just as was done for the single diamond cell from the *Origami* design. Many of these expanded patterns look busy, but some very interesting patterns can be developed by experimenting in this fashion.

Primary cell

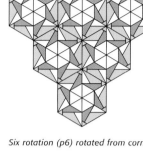

Spinning Sunflower

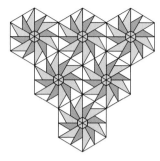

Six rotation (p6) rotated from corner A

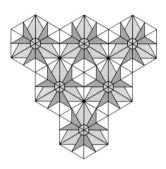

Six rotation (p6) rotated from corner B

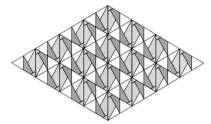

Midpoint rotation (p2)

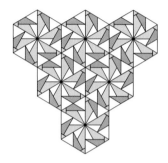

Six rotation (p6) rotated from corner C

Mirror and three rotations (p3m1)

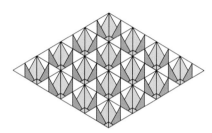

Staggered mirror (cm), mirrored on side AC

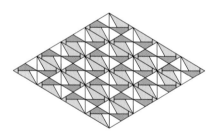

Staggered mirror (cm), mirrored on side BC

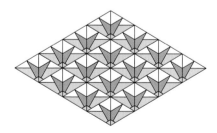

Staggered mirror (cm), mirrored on side AB

Illustration 6.7. *Eight patterns created from an equilateral triangle cell.*

Working with an Equilateral Triangle Primary Cell

The equilateral triangle was used to illustrate how to create patterns in the mirror and three rotations (p3m1) symmetry and the six rotation (p6) symmetry groups. Three patterns occur with the p6 symmetry as each angle can be rotated to produce a different design. I have found four additional patterns that can be generated with the triangle by applying some of the other symmetry operations. The triangle can be midpoint rotated (p2) to create one pattern or a staggered mirror (cm) can be applied on each of the sides to create three additional patterns. With midpoint rotation, the same pattern occurs no matter which side is rotated. With the staggered mirror, three different patterns occur depending on which side is mirrored. Note that the triangle can also be glided, but the glide produces exactly the same patterns as the mirror.

The design *Spinning Sunflower* is an example of six rotation (p6) symmetry. The primary cell is an equilateral triangle. Six cells have been rotated around one of the corners to create this design. Illustration 6.7 shows the design plus the other seven patterns that can be created from the same cell.

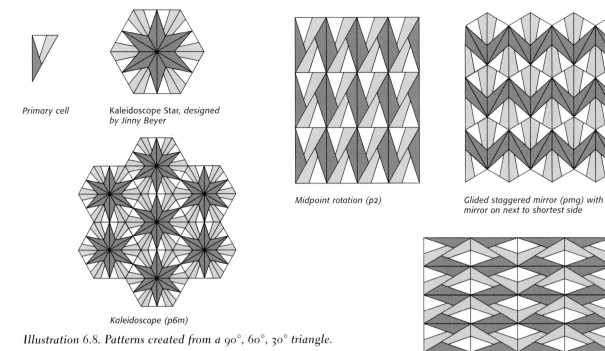

Primary cell

Kaleidoscope Star, *designed by Jinny Beyer*

Kaleidoscope (p6m)

Midpoint rotation (p2)

Glided staggered mirror (pmg) with mirror on next to shortest side

Illustration 6.8. Patterns created from a 90°, 60°, 30° triangle.

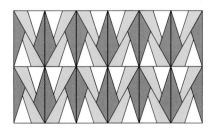

Glided staggered mirror with mirror on shortest side (pmg)

Glided staggered mirror (pmg) with mirror on longest side

Staggered double mirror (cmm)

Working with a 90°, 60°, 30° Triangle Primary Cell

A 90°, 60°, 30° triangle is the shape used as a primary cell in the kaleidoscope (p6m) symmetry group. For that symmetry the triangle is mirrored and then rotated six times. However, I have found three additional symmetry operations that can also be applied to the cell to create five additional patterns. These are midpoint rotation (p2); glided staggered mirror (pmg), which produces three patterns; and staggered double mirror (cmm). These are shown in Illustration 6.8.

Once again many additional patterns are possible if the primary cells are grouped into a rectangle and then the various symmetry operations applied.

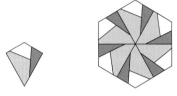

Primary cell

Pinwheel, designed by Jinny Beyer

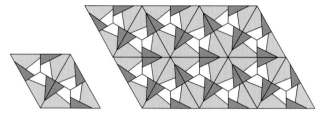

Tile

Three rotations and a mirror (p31m)

Working with a Kite-Shaped Primary Cell

There are only four patterns I have found that can be created from a kite-shaped primary cell. Two of them were discussed in Chapter 4. Those are patterns in the three rotations and a mirror (p31m) and six rotation (p6) symmetry groups. The kite shape can also be used to generate a pattern in two other ways: with a midpoint rotation (p2) and with a glide (pg).

The primary cell from the *Pinwheel* design is shown here, along with the four patterns that can be created from the same primary cell. Shading the primary cell in different ways also alters the appearance of the patterns.

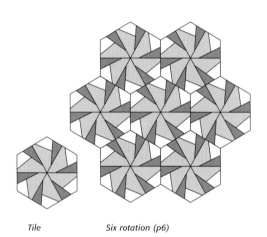

Tile

Six rotation (p6)

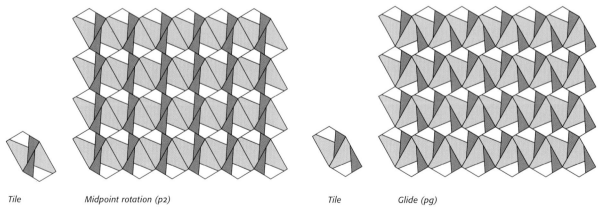

Tile

Midpoint rotation (p2)

Tile

Glide (pg)

Illustration 6.9. Patterns created from a kite-shaped cell.

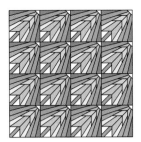

Primary cell   *Translation (p1)*

Illustration 6.10. Translation (p1) symmetry applied to Lone Pine.

Applying Symmetry Operations to an Already Symmetrical Design

Isolating the primary cell in a design and applying the various symmetry operation to that cell is not the only way to generate new patterns from an existing design. The entire design can have symmetry motion applied to it, opening the door for even more patterns. In other words after the tile is created, instead of translating that tile over and over, apply some of the other symmetry movements to the tile. An example of this is shown in the *Lone Pine* design (Illustration 6.10). *Lone Pine* is an example of staggered mirror (cm) symmetry when the tile is simply translated, but it can look very different when some of the other symmetry operations are applied to the tile, as shown in Illustration 6.11. Note when using this technique that since the design you are beginning with has symmetry within the tile, some of the symmetries, when applied, will produce the same pattern.

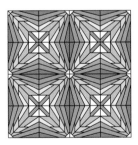

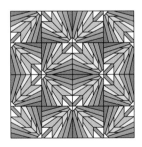

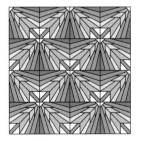

Traditional block (p4m), double mirror (pmm), pinwheel (p4), rotated from corners along mirror line of cell, mirrored pinwheel (p4g).

Mirrored pinwheel (p4g) when rotated from non-mirrored corners.

Double glide (pgg), pinwheel (p4) when rotated from non-mirrored side.

Staggered mirror (cm).

Illustration 6.11. Some additional symmetries applied to Lone Pine.

Primary cell

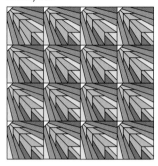
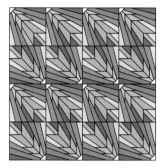

Translation (p1)   *Midpoint rotation (p2)*   *Double mirror (pmm)*   *Staggered double mirror (cmm)*

Illustration 6.12. Nonsymmetrical coloring of Lone Pine.

Illustration 6.13. Mirrored pinwheel (p4g) symmetry with Lone Pine.

Even more patterns can be generated if the symmetrical design is colored in a nonsymmetrical way. In Illustration 6.12 *Lone Pine* has been colored nonsymmetrically. You can apply all 11 symmetry operations that work with a square (at least 28 different patterns) to that asymmetrical unit. A few examples are shown.

Yet another way to create new patterns from an existing design is to divide the block into new primary cells. For example, in Illustration 6.13 the asymmetrically colored *Lone Pine* design has been divided in two ways to create four completely different triangular units. At least six different patterns could be created from each one by applying the various symmetry operations that work with a right triangle. The mirrored pinwheel (p4g) symmetry is illustrated here with each of the four triangles. Instead of dividing the design into triangular units, you could divide it into four smaller squares and apply the symmetries to each

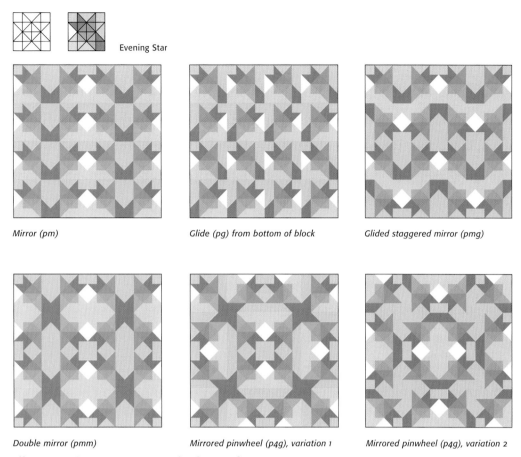

Evening Star

Mirror (pm)   Glide (pg) from bottom of block   Glided staggered mirror (pmg)

Double mirror (pmm)   Mirrored pinwheel (p4g), variation 1   Mirrored pinwheel (p4g), variation 2

Illustration 6.14. Nonsymmetrical coloring of Evening Star.

of those squares. As you can see, the possibilities for design are endless.

The *Evening Star* design is another traditional quilt block. Just like *Lone Pine* in Illustration 6.12, it can be colored in a nonsymmetrical way. Several of the 28 possible patterns I have found that can be created by applying the different symmetries are shown in Illustration 6.14.

Exercise 4

Designing with Asymmetrical Shapes

1. The shapes shown here have marks at the same intervals along the sides that will join together. Divide each shape so that lines will come to those marks on the sides. Make sure, however, that you divide the shape in an asymmetrical way so that you have a primary cell. A sample design for each shape is shown. See how many other designs you can create for these shapes using the same markings. Try photocopying just line drawings of your cell or add value differences. 2. Photocopy your designs in regular and reverse images and apply all the applicable symmetries to them.

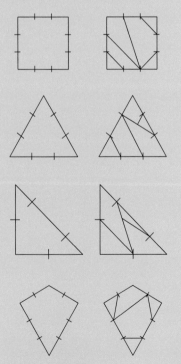

Designing Your Own Primary Cell

Rather than working with a preexisting design, it can be fun to design your own primary cell and then apply the various symmetry motions to it. Begin with one of the shapes discussed so far, draw various lines on it, shade it in, and apply the symmetries that are applicable to that shape. Many different interesting patterns will result.

Something I try to achieve when designing my own primary cells, is to have the lines that I draw within the cell come to the edges of the shape at the same places on all sides. That way when the cell is translated, flipped, mirrored, and rotated, the lines will continue from one cell to the next in a uniformly flowing pattern. When working with a square cell, an underlying grid made up of a certain number of smaller squares works well. When working with other shapes, the sides of the shapes that will touch need to be divided equally. To visualize this, look at the two cells shown in Illustration 6.15. Both are very similar, but you can see from the underlying grid, which is made up of nine squares, that the lines on the design in the top row do not follow the grid, whereas the ones in the second row do.

When applying symmetry motions to the two cells, you can see that the patterns on the left look ragged and disjointed, whereas the ones on the right have more unity. I often find when creating these patterns, the lines forming the outline of the shape of the cell interfere with the design. Sometimes I eliminate the outline and just let the internal lines dictate the design. The designs at the bottom of Illustration 6.15 show the basic design with the outlining square eliminated.

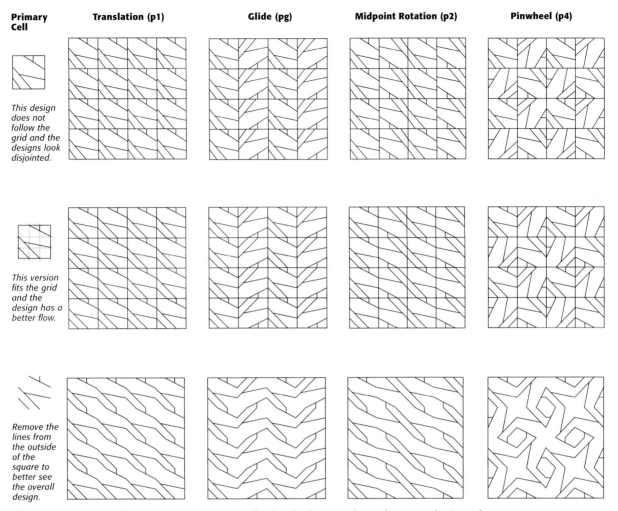

Illustration 6.15. Applying symmetries to two cells. On the bottom, the outlines are eliminated.

A general rule of thumb to keep in mind if you design your own primary cell is that no matter what shape you begin with, the sides of that shape that will be adjacent to each other should have lines coming to the same places and at equal distance on those sides. This is not to say that you will not achieve interesting designs if you do otherwise; but you may have more success if you follow these general guidelines.

Illustration 6.16. Are faces symmetrical? The photographs of Abraham Lincoln, Edgar Allan Poe, and Vivien Leigh are cut in half, straight down the middle. Look what happens when the left sides and right sides of the faces are mirrored.

Illustration 6.17. Cats faces seem more symmetrical than the faces of people. See how perfectly the left and right sides align here.

Symmetry Breaking

A study of the photo images in Chapter 2 will show that in nature symmetry is imperfect. The two wings of a butterfly are not exactly the same. A reflection in a pond or lake is always less perfect than the image it is duplicating. Two halves of a leaf, the petals on a flower, a snowflake, both sides of a human face—all are expected to be symmetrical, therefore our mind sees them that way. But the fact that there are slight discrepancies makes them even more beautiful and interesting to look at than if all parts were exactly the same. Symmetry breaking, then, is what happens when symmetry is *expected* but certain discrepancies interrupt the pattern. The mind's eye fills in the places where the expectation is not met.

The photographs shown here illustrate examples of perfect symmetry as well as examples of symmetry breaking.

Illustration 6.18. The seemingly perfectly symmetrical face of the dog is broken—the tongue hangs to one side.

Illustration 6.19. At first glance, one would think both designs were symmetrical, but a closer look shows breaks in each symmetry. On the left, ceiling of the Amber Palace, India; on the right, glazed earthenware by Bernard Palissy, France, 16th century.

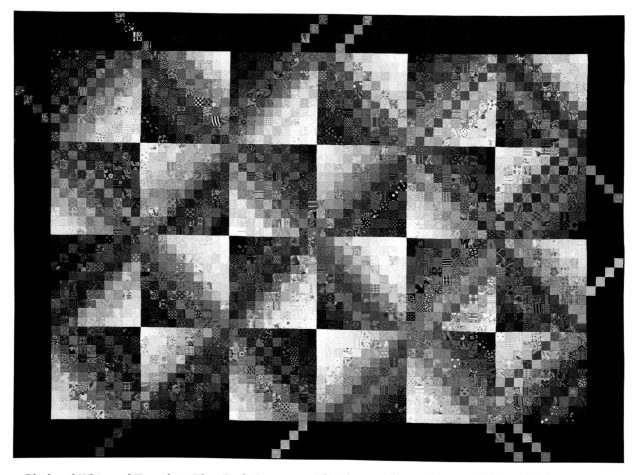

Black and White and Everything Else, *Gayle Ropp, 1997. This charm quilt contains 2,444 different fabrics.*

Symmetry breaking occurs all the time in nature when there are areas that interrupt the symmetry, giving individualism to each item. Symmetry can be soothing and comforting, but too much perfection can also become boring, cold, and uninviting. When using the guidelines of symmetry to create a pattern, whether it be weaving, quilting, painting, or other surface design, bear in mind that breaking the symmetry now and then can sometimes result in a more intriguing pattern.

Black and White and Everything Else is a good example of symmetry breaking. The designer created blocks made up of small squares. The squares are organized within the blocks so that they shade from light to dark diagonally. But the shading and coloring is not exactly the same in each block. Each square is cut from a different fabric and the designer used a total of 2,444 different prints. The blocks were put together in a double glide

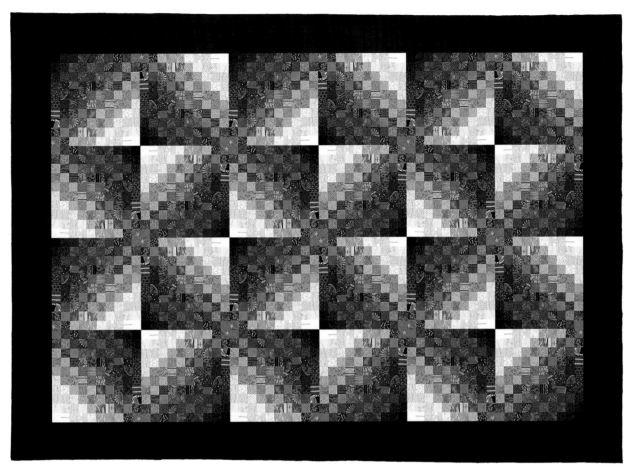

Illustration 6.20. Computer-generated version of Black and White and Everything Else, *using the same double glide (pgg) symmetry as the original quilt, but with all blocks exactly the same.*

(pgg) symmetry. Yes, there is a calmness and unity because of the symmetrical placement of the blocks, but it is the different fabrics that were used, the slight variations in the value changes within the blocks, and the interesting border that make this quilt intriguing. Compare this quilt with the computer-generated one in Illustration 6.20 where all of the blocks have been made exactly the same.

Enchanted Forest, *Jinny Beyer, 1995.*
Three symmetry motions (translation, mirror, and rotation) were used to
transform a rectangle into the tessellating pattern of this quilt. The quilt
is an example of glided staggered mirror (pmg) symmetry.

CHAPTER 7

The Keys to Creating
Interlocking Tessellations

CHAPTER 1 GAVE A BRIEF INTRODUCTION to
tessellations, and Chapter 2 through Chapter 6
explained in detail the principles of one- and two-
dimensional symmetry on which they depend. We
can now go on to explain tessellations and to see
how understanding symmetry makes it easier to
design and analyze tessellating motifs. Once you
become excited about tessellations, the temp-
tation to begin designing for your own medium
right away can be irresistible. However, I urge you
to read through this chapter first, do the exercises,
and try to keep thoughts of your own designs out
of your mind. Just learn the concepts. Practice
them. The next chapters will show ways of applying what you have learned to your own area of
interest.

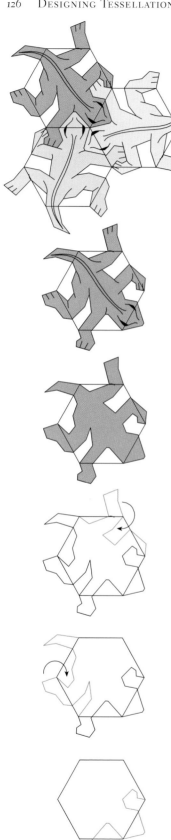

Creating Interlocking Shapes

A close look at some of the notes and sketches in M. C. Escher's notebooks shows that there is an underlying grid on most of his designs. The way to determine the grid is to draw lines between the places where the various motifs join. That underlying grid shows the repeating tile and the primary cell, and once those are determined it is easier to see the symmetry that is used for the repeating pattern.

The question comes, however, of how to create some of these interlocking motifs in the first place. As explained earlier, shapes such as a triangle, quadrilateral, or hexagon are tessellations as they will fit together side by side and fill a space without gaps or overlaps. If a piece is taken away from one of those shapes, that shape will no longer fit together without gaps, and therefore it is no longer a tessellation. If, however, the piece that was taken away is *given back to another side of the shape*, then once again there is a tessellation (see Illustration 1.4 on page 4).

Illustration 1.5 on page 5 provides 20 designs that were all created from a square, and the same piece was cut out of the square

Symmetry Drawing E25 (*Reptiles*) *by* M. C. Escher.

for each of the designs. The only difference was in how that piece was given back and which symmetry was used to complete the pattern. There are several ways a piece that has been removed from a shape can be given back to create an interlocking design, and they are all based on the same four principles of symmetry — translation, rotation, glide, and mirror. There are various rules as to what will and will not work, and these vary depending upon the shape being used. There is, however, a universal rule: *when a piece is taken out of one side of a shape, the side it is given back to must be of equal length.* Each of the methods for creating tessellations will be discussed in detail in the following pages.

Once an interlocking shape has been created, multiples of the shape will fit together to form the overall pattern. Just as in the symmetry examples, tiles or translation units made up of one or more of the tessellating shapes can be repeated over and over by translation to form the pattern. How many of the motifs are required to create the repeating tile depends on the way the shape was transformed.

Heesch Labeling System

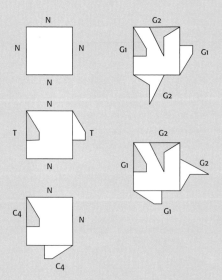

As each of the four methods for creating tessellating motifs is explained, a revised form of a labeling system developed by German mathematician Heinrich Heesch will be used. It was published in 1963 in *Flachenschluss*, a book he coauthored with Otto Kienzle. In this system, a label is given to each operation that is performed on the sides of a shape. T = translation, G = glide, C (center of rotation) = midpoint or half-turn (180°) rotation, $C3$ = 120° rotation, $C4$ = quarter-turn or 90° rotation, and $C6$ = 60° rotation. Used alone, G = glide. I have taken the liberty of adding an M (mirror) and an N (no changes) to that labeling system as well, because many designs can be changed by mirroring one of the sides. There are also times when no changes at all are made.

In the labeling system, the letter given to each side of the shape depends on what operation was performed. Those letters appear in a clockwise order. For instance a square with no changes would be labeled *NNNN*. A square with a translation from one side to another, but with no changes on the other two sides would be labeled *NTNT*, a square with a rotation from one side to an adjacent side, but with no other changes would be labeled NNC_4C_4, and so on.

With translation, you always know which side was translated to the other, because only opposite and parallel sides can be translated. But with most shapes a glide can occur from one side of the shape to any other side of equal length, therefore when more than one glide occurs, a number has to be used as well. *G1* and *G2* are used where more than one glide is performed on the same shape. For instance with a square, *G1*, *G2*, *G1*, *G2* would have the glides occurring on opposite sides. *G1*, *G1*, *G2*, *G2* would have the glides occurring on adjacent sides of the square. You will always know that the piece cut out of a side labeled *G1*, was given back to the other side that is also labeled *G1*.

Quadrilaterals (shapes with four sides)

1 90° 90° 90° 90°
TTTT
TCTC
CCCC
C4C4C4C4
C4C4MM
G1G1G2G2
TGTG
CCGG
CGCG

2 90° 90° 90° 90°
TTTT
CCCC
TCTC
TGTG
GCGC
TCTM

3 120° 90° 90° 60°
CCCC
G1G1G2G2
C3C3C6C6

4 45° 120° 120° 45°
TTTT
CCCC
TCTC

5 60° 120° 120° 60°
TTTT   G1G1G2G2
CCCC   GGCC
TCTC   C3C3C3C3
TGTG   GCGC

6 120° 120° 60° 60°
CCCC   GNGM
GNGN   CCCM
GCGC   C3C3NN
GGNN

Triangles (shapes with three sides)

7 30° 30° 60°
C3C3C   CCC
C3C3M   CCM
GGC   GGM

8 60° 60° 60°
CC6C6
CCC
GGC
GGM

9 45° 90° 45°
MMM
CC4C4
GGM   C4C4M
CMM   GGC
CCC

10 60° 60° 30°
GGM
CCC
GGC

11 30° 60° 90°
CMM
CCC
MMM
CCM

Hexagons (shapes with six sides)

12 120° 120° 120° 120° 120° 120°
TTTTT
TCCTCC
C3C3C3C3C3C3
TG1G1TG2G2
TG1G2TG2TG1
TCCTGG

13 90° 120° 120° 120° 120° 90°
TTTTTT
TCCTCC
TG1TG1TG2TG2
TG1G2TG2TG1

Pentagons (shapes with five sides)

14 120° 120° 60°
C6C6NNN
C6C6C3C3N

15 90° 90°
C4C4C4CC
C4C4C4C4N

Labeling System

The notations inside these shapes show many of the transformations that can be applied to the shapes that will allow them to form interlocking motifs.

T = **Translation** Translations can only move a piece from one side of the shape to an opposite, parallel side of equal length.

G = **Glide** In a glide the piece is flipped and moved from one side of the shape to another side of the shape that is equal in length. G1 and G2 are used where more than one glide is done in the same shape. G1 corresponds to G1, and G2 corresponds to G2.

C = **Rotation (Center of Rotation)** This is a midpoint rotation on one of the sides of the shape (180° rotation).

C3 = **Rotation Around a 120° Angle** The piece is rotated from one side of the shape around a 120° angle to an adjacent side of equal length.

C4 = **Rotation Around a 90° Angle** The rotation is done around a 90° angle from one side of the shape to an adjacent side of equal length.

C6 = **Rotation Around a 60° Angle** The rotation is done around a 60° angle from one side of the shape to an adjacent side of equal length.

M = **Mirror** The shape is flipped or mirrored along an unaltered side.

N = **None** No change has taken place.

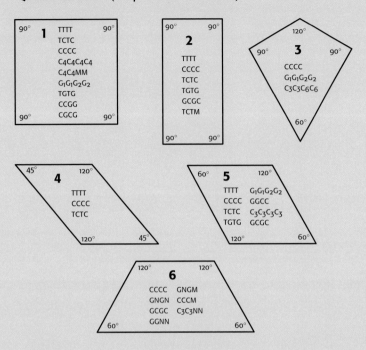
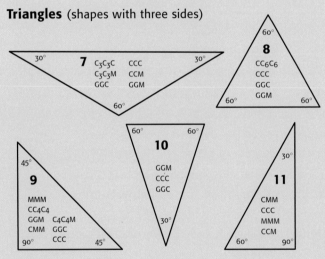
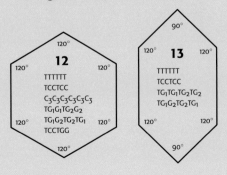
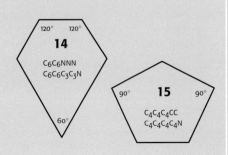

An Easy Experiment

I find one of the easiest ways to experiment with tessellations is to work with 3″ × 5″ lined index cards. Cut the shapes out of those cards, perform the various operations, and tape the piece that was cut onto one of the other sides. Lined cards help because when working with operations that require a flip of the piece before it is given back, the lines on that piece will indicate that you have given it back correctly and that you will also have to flip the completed shape back and forth when drawing around it.

It should be noted, however, that cutting a chunk out of the side of a shape is not the only way to create a tessellation. The shape can also be altered both within and outside of the line, as illustrated here. Tracing paper can be used to experiment with this method, and even though tracing paper is more cumbersome to use, it offers more versatility. When working on tracing paper you can draw both within and outside the shape, then you can move the paper to the side in which the piece will be given back and trace it onto that side. No matter which way you choose, the designs will still tessellate.

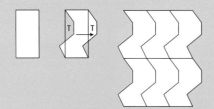

The piece does not always have to be cut within the shape. The piece that is translated can go both inside and outside the original shape.

Translation

The first method of creating interlocking tessellating motifs is by translation. With translation a piece is cut out of one side of the shape and is moved directly across to the opposite side. In translation a piece can only be moved from one side of the shape to a side that is parallel and also equal in length. This then limits the shapes that can be used for translation and leads to a second universal rule: *translation can only be done on squares, rectangles, parallelograms, or hexagons that have parallel sides that are equal in length.* Illustration 7.1 shows how a translation is performed on a square, hexagon, and parallelogram and what those shapes look like when several are put together. Note the use of the Heesch labeling system, as explained on page 128. Notice that when multiples of the shape are put together to create the pattern, the piece is not rotated or flipped. It is oriented in the same direction at all times and simply translated side by side for the pattern. With translation only one cell or motif makes up the repeating tile.

Additional translations can be performed on a shape as long as there are remaining sides that are equal in length and parallel to each other. For example, Illustration 7.2 shows the same shapes, but now two more sides have been altered. In the case of the hexagon, there are still two unaltered sides that are parallel to each other, and those can be translated as well.

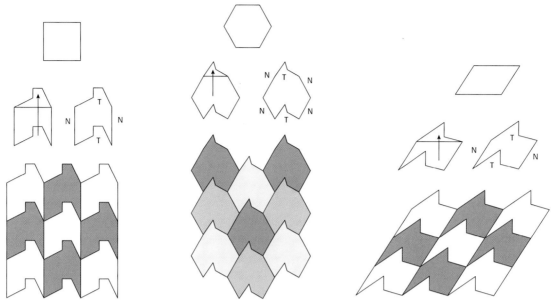

Illustration 7.1. Translation performed on a square, hexagon, and parallelogram.

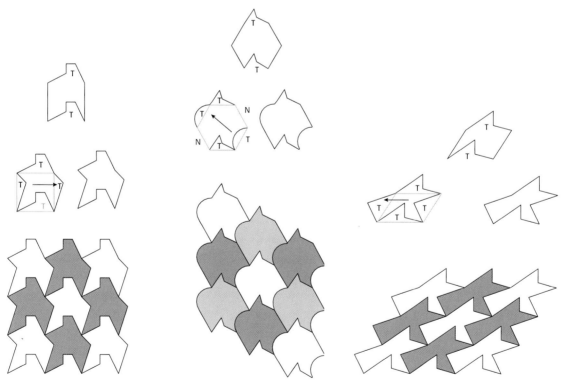

Illustration 7.2. Two more sides are altered.

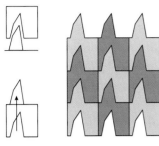

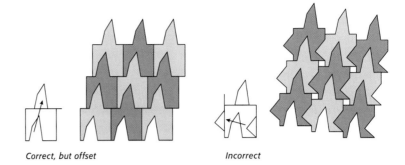

Correct

Correct, but offset   Incorrect

With a quadrilateral, if one side is not translated straight across, the pieces will still fit together without gaps, but if the translation on the next side is also offset, the pieces will not fit together without gaps.

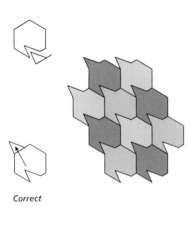

Correct

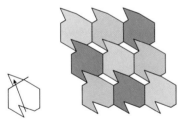

Incorrect

With a hexagon, the piece must be translated straight across or there will be gaps. If the piece is not cut corner to corner, you have to make sure to move it straight across. Imagine a hairline that extends to the corners. That hairline cannot extend over the edges, or you run the risk, depending on the shape, that the pieces will not fit together without gaps.

Illustration 7.3. Tessellations put together without gaps or overlaps.

For experimentation and learning it is best to alter corner to corner the whole side of the shape instead of cutting a piece out of only one portion of the side. Either way will work, but since it is more difficult to move the piece exactly straight across to the opposite side it is easy to get into problems when cutting only a part of the side. It might shift just a little to one side or the other. You have to imagine that there is a tiny hairline extending to the corners from the piece that was cut. As that piece is translated, if it is not moved exactly straight across, the hairline will extend out over the edge of the piece. When working with translation of a square, rectangle, or parallelogram, shapes would still fit together; they would just be off-set. But with a hexagon the shapes would not fit together at all. Furthermore, on the square and rectangle if the remaining two sides were translated with a slight shift instead of straight across, they would not fit together without a gap, as shown in Illustration 7.3.

The following photographs and illustrations show examples of three tessellating designs that were created by translation. All of these are examples of translation (p1) symmetry. In all cases, the primary cell is the altered shape. One motif makes up the tile, which is translated over and over for the pattern.

The first example is *Pelican Migration*, Illustration 7.4. The designer began with a square and translated all four sides. Lines were drawn to any inward angles to make the shape easier for sewing, ending up with four pattern pieces. Each pelican was cut from a different fabric.

The second example is in Escher's design, *Flying Fish*. You can see in Illustration 7.5 how the underlying shape is a parallelogram and how translations were done on all four sides.

The third example, Illustration 7.6, is a graphic design that I created by beginning with a hexagon and translating three of the sides to their opposite parallel sides.

Pelican Migration, *Kathryn Kuhn, 1993.*

Kathryn began with a square and took a piece out of the top and translated it to the bottom.

Next a piece was taken from the left side and translated to the right side.

To make it easier to sew, she broke the shape into four pieces by adding lines from any inward angles on the shape. For each individual pelican those four pieces were cut from the same fabric.

Illustration 7.4. Creating Pelican Migration.

Begin with a parallelogram.   *Translate left side to right side.*   *Translate to bottom.*

Illustration 7.5. Symmetry Drawing E73 (Flying Fish) by M. C. Escher.

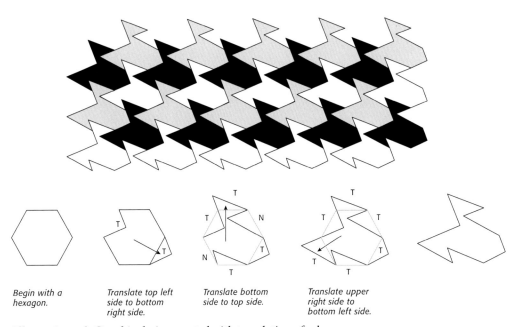

Begin with a hexagon.   *Translate top left side to bottom right side.*   *Translate bottom side to top side.*   *Translate upper right side to bottom left side.*

Illustration 7.6. Graphic design created with translation of a hexagon.

Exercise 5

Altered Shapes Translated

Refer to the numbered shape sheet shown here and indicate which shapes
can be altered by translation. Also indicate how many of the sides of the
shape can be altered by translation. The answers can be found in Appendix C.

Quadrilaterals (shapes with four sides)

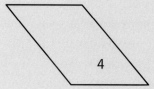

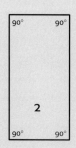

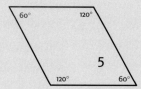

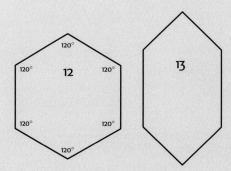

Triangles (shapes with three sides)

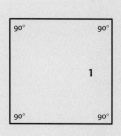

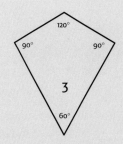

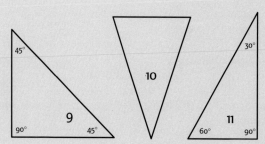

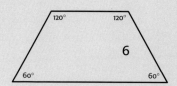

Hexagons (shapes with six sides)

Pentagons (shapes with five sides)

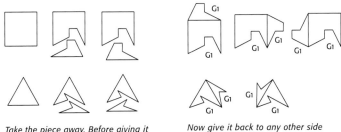

Take the piece away. Before giving it back, flip it.

Now give it back to any other side that is equal in length.

Illustration 7.7. Glide performed on a square and a triangle.

Glided motif

Glided motif is flipped and turned before given back.

Tile

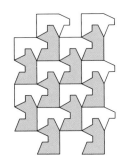

Illustration 7.8. Creating the repeating tile.

Glide

The second method of creating tessellating shapes is with a glide. You will recall from studying the symmetries that the primary cell for the glide (pg) symmetry was moved and flipped. The same holds true with creating a glided tessellating motif. After the piece is taken away from the shape, before it is given back, it is flipped. That is one of the differences between translated tessellating motifs and ones that are glided. The second difference between the two is that with a glide, the piece can be given back to any side of the shape as long as that side is of equal length. The side that the piece is given back to does not have to be parallel. This offers much more diversity of design and allows shapes other than the quadrilateral or hexagon to be used as well.

To create a glided tessellating design, take the piece out of one side of the shape and then flip it before giving it back. Once

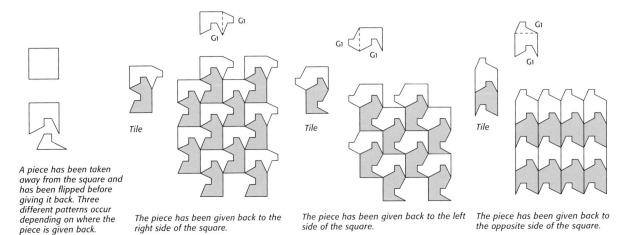

A piece has been taken away from the square and has been flipped before giving it back. Three different patterns occur depending on where the piece is given back.

The piece has been given back to the right side of the square.

Tile

The piece has been given back to the left side of the square.

Tile

The piece has been given back to the opposite side of the square.

Tile

Illustration 7.9. Three glided designs from same piece cut from a square.

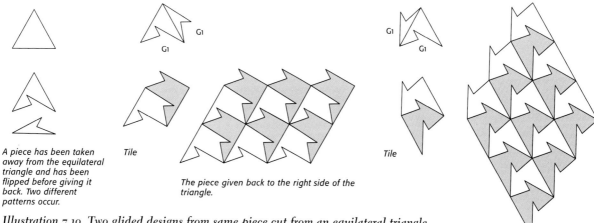

A piece has been taken away from the equilateral triangle and has been flipped before giving it back. Two different patterns occur.

Tile

The piece given back to the right side of the triangle.

Illustration 7.10. Two glided designs from same piece cut from an equilateral triangle.

Tile

The piece given back to the left side of the triangle.

the piece has been flipped, then it can be given back to any side of the shape that is equal in length. If it is moved straight across such as can be done with a square or parallelogram, the piece will not have to be turned, but if it is given back to one of the adjacent sides, then in addition to being flipped it must also be turned so that the straight edge on the cut piece can be put against the straight edge on the new side (Illustration 7.7).

This time when joining multiple shapes to create the pattern, the motif must be alternately flipped in order for it to fit together. I find it easiest to create the tile first and then just repeat the tile over and over by translation without any further flips or turns of the pieces. In most cases only two cells are required to create the repeating tile. The exception to this is when two glides are performed on opposite sides of a parallelogram. Then four cells will be needed for the repeating tile.

Illustration 7.9 shows three different glided designs created with the same piece cut from the bottom side of the square, and Illustration 7.10 shows two different designs where the same piece has been cut from an equilateral triangle. The difference in how the design looks depends on which side of the the shape the piece is given back—in the case of the squares, the opposite side, the right side, or the left side and in the case of the triangle, one of the two remaining sides.

Once two sides of a parallelogram have been glided, the other two sides can be glided as well to create even more design possibilities. The same glided squares have now been used again with the additional sides glided (Illustration 7.11). In each case the same shaped piece has been cut from one of the remaining sides. You can see how quickly the designs are changed. Imagine

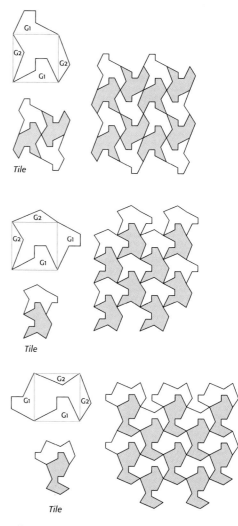

Tile

Tile

Tile

Illustration 7.11. Additional sides of a square are glided.

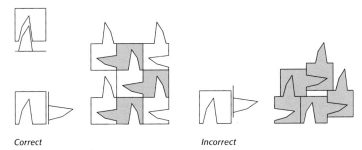

Correct   Incorrect

Create a hairline that extends to the corners of the shape, and use this as a guide to position the glided piece of the motif so it will fill the surface without gaps or overlaps.

Illustration 7.12.

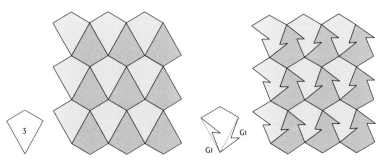

If the shape can be flipped (glided) and fill the surface without any gaps, then a piece can also be cut from the shape and glided and the result will fill the surface, as in shape 3.

Illustration 7.13.

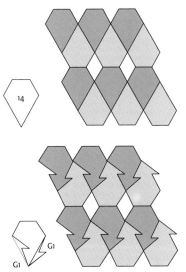

If the shape is flipped and will not fill the surface without gaps, then a piece cannot be cut from the shape and glided. There will be a gap, as in shape 14.

Illustration 7.14.

how much more they can change when the piece that is cut is altered in even small ways. In each case the repeating tiles or translation units are shown along with the pattern. Keep in mind that when the glides are done to opposite sides of the parallelogram four cells are needed for the repeating tiles, but when it is done to adjacent sides, only two cells are needed for the repeating tile.

The hairline that was discussed in the translation section above is also a very important factor when dealing with a glide, but it can be a little confusing when doing the flip of the piece that has been taken away. In other words, if a piece is not taken away from corner to corner of the shape, but from only part of the side, you have to imagine that the hairline extends all the way to the corners of the shape, so that when the piece is flipped and given back to another side, it will go back in the proper place. You have to visualize that the piece that is taken away has a hinge on it right at the center of the side of the shape. The piece has to flip along that hinge line. If the piece is off by even a small amount, the shapes will not fit together as shown in Illustration 7.12.

A question may arise. Which of the shapes on page 135 can have a glide applied to them and still tessellate, filling the space without any gaps or overlaps, and which cannot? How can you know ahead of time before making any alterations to the shape?

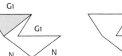

Begin with a parallelogram.

Take a piece away from one side, flip it, and give it back to an adjacent side.

Add a line to make it easy to break up the shape.

Tile

Arriving at an answer is easy. Make two of the shapes in question. Determine which side you want to cut the piece out of, flip one of the shapes upside down and fit the two together along the sides that will have the piece cut away. Tape these two together. If you can draw around them and fill the surface without any gaps or overlaps, you will be able to perform a glide on the shape and have it tessellate as well.

Let us say for example that you want to do a glide on the long edges of shapes 3 and 14 from page 135, cutting a piece out of one of the long sides, flipping it, and giving it back to the other long side. When each of those shapes is put together before any alterations are done you will see that shape 3 will fill the plane without any gaps or overlaps and shape 14 will not (Illustrations 7.13 and 7.14). If a shape does not tessellate when a glide is performed on the unaltered shape, it will not tessellate in an interlocking manner after the shape is altered with a glide, as can be seen in both illustrations.

Shapes that have only one glide performed on them are of the glide (pg) symmetry. Parallelograms that have two glides performed to opposite sides are of the double glide (pgg) symmetry.

Two examples of designs created with glide symmetry are shown. The first, in Illustration 7.15, is a graphic design suitable for a textile design, a quilt pattern, or other applications. The second one is a quilt, *Strip T's*.

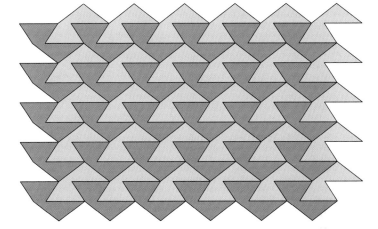

This design could easily be sewn in fabric by making the shape two pieces instead of one. Both pieces could be cut from the same fabric so that the individual shapes would still stand out.

Illustration 7.15. A simple tessellation from a parallelogram.

Exercise 6

Altering Shapes with Glide

Refer to the numbered shape sheet shown on page 135 and indicate which shapes can be glided. Also indicate how many of the sides of the shape can be altered by a glide.

The answers can be found in Appendix C.

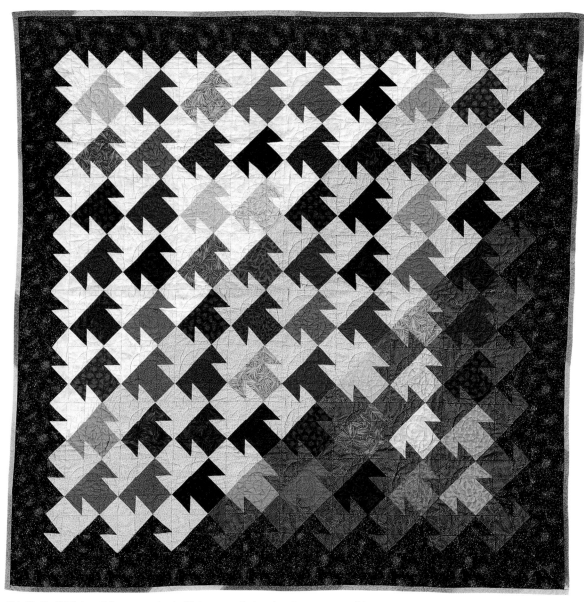

Strip T's, *Terri Willet, 1998, is an example of glided staggered mirror (pmg) symmetry. A glide was performed on a square to create the tessellating design.*

  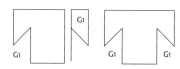

Begin with a square.

Take a piece away from one of the sides. Remember the hairline joint to the corner.

Flip the piece vertically, and give it back to the opposite side.

To use this design in a quilt, the shape would have to be broken down into three pieces. They could all be done in the same fabric so the T's would still stand out.

Illustration 7.16. A simple tessellation from a square is the basis of Strip T's.

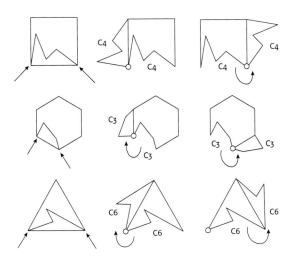

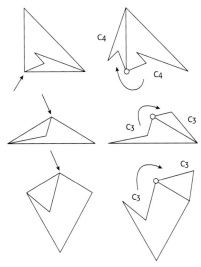

On these shapes the rotation can occur on two different angles because the adjacent sides are equal in length to the side from which the piece was cut.

Illustration 7.17. Rotation around a corner.

On these shapes the rotation can occur around only one of the angles because there is only one adjacent side that is equal in length to the side from which the piece was cut.

Rotation

The third method of creating tessellating motifs is by rotation. Rotation is different from glide and translation in that it can occur in two ways. With either of the two types of rotation, the piece that is cut is rotated a certain number of degrees, depending on the shape. It is as though the piece that is cut never lets go of the main shape, but rather that it has a hinge at the point of rotation.

The first type of rotation is similar to the others in that the piece is cut out of one side of the shape and is given back to another side. There are limits, however, as to which side the piece can be given back. It must be rotated around the corner to an adjacent side of equal length (Illustration 7.17).

Second, rotation can be performed on a single side of the shape (midpoint rotation). In this case the piece is cut out of part of the side and rotated 180° at the midpoint of the side and then given back to the same side (Illustration 7.18). It is easiest to see this type of rotation if the piece is cut from half of the side and rotated to the other half, but it is not necessary to do this to perform the operation. As long as the piece is rotated at the midpoint of the side, it can be cut

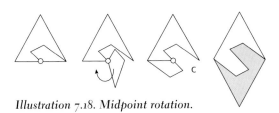

Illustration 7.18. Midpoint rotation.

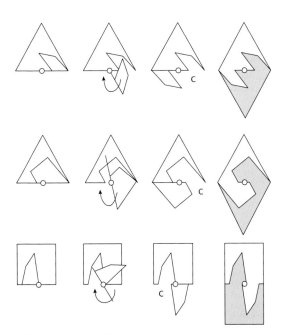

Illustration 7.19 Three examples of midpoint rotation.

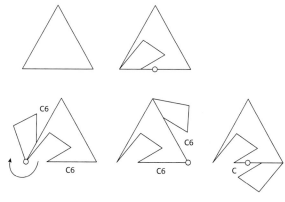

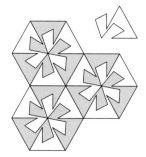 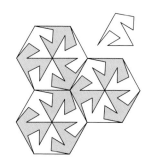

Rotated to the left   *Rotated to the right*   *Midpoint rotated*

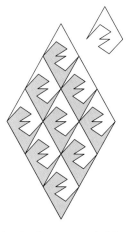

The same piece has been cut out of all three triangles, yet because of where the rotation occurs, all three patterns look very different.

Illustration 7.20. Patterns differ depending on how the rotation occurs.

from anywhere along that side as shown in Illustration 7.19. Midpoint rotation is a very important transformation to remember as this technique can alter a single side of the shape. When working with triangles, once two sides of the shape have been altered by a rotation or a glide, the only two possible ways to change the last side are by mirroring (which only works on certain shapes) and midpoint rotation.

As you can see in Illustration 7.19, the hairline that was discussed in the translation and glide sections is equally important when dealing with a rotation. If a piece is cut out of only a portion of the side but is still going to be rotated around the corner or along the same side, there must be an imaginary hairline connecting that piece to the corner. The whole side of the piece must be rotated, not just the section that was taken away.

Illustration 7.20 shows a triangle with a piece cut out of part of one of the sides. It shows that piece rotated around the 60° angle to the left side and around the 60° angle to the right side. Next the piece is midpoint rotated to the same side of the shape. You can see how different the pattern is depending on how the rotation occurs.

Center of Rotation

The use of the letter *C* in Heesch's system can be confusing if you don't understand what the numbers stand for. *C* stands for "center of rotation." When the rotation is done to a single side of a shape (midpoint rotation), the letter *C* alone is used. C3 is used when the rotation is done around an angle of 120°. (It takes three shapes to complete the tile, or three rotations to complete 360°.) C4 is used when the rotation is done around an angle of 90°. (It takes four shapes to form the tile, or four rotations to complete 360°.) C6 is used when the rotation is done around an angle of 60°. (It takes six shapes to form the tile, and six rotations to complete 360°.)

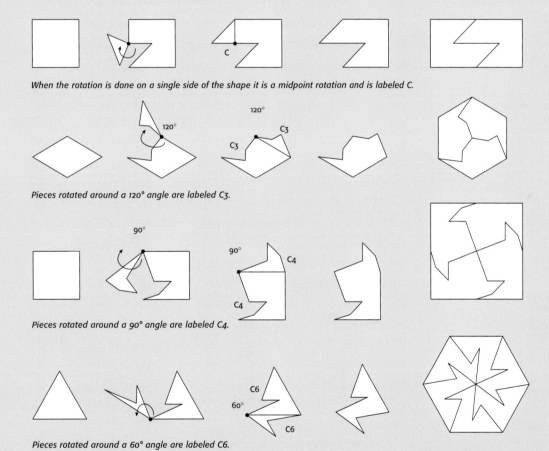

When the rotation is done on a single side of the shape it is a midpoint rotation and is labeled C.

Pieces rotated around a 120° angle are labeled C3.

Pieces rotated around a 90° angle are labeled C4.

Pieces rotated around a 60° angle are labeled C6.

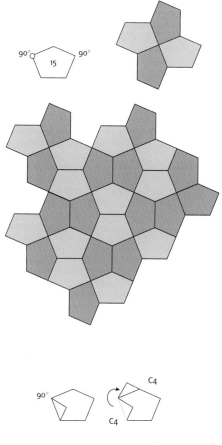

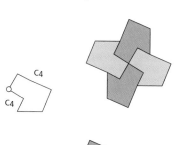

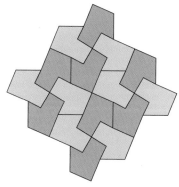

If the unaltered shape rotates around the angle and fills the surface without any gaps, then it will also fill the surface when a piece is taken away and rotated around that same corner.

Illustration 7.21.

Rotation for creating tessellating motifs is just the same as rotation in the layout of the various symmetries in that it can only be performed on shapes with either 60°, 90°, or 120° angles. When rotation is performed, the angle around which the rotation occurs determines the number of cells required to form the repeating tile. Rotation around a 60° angle requires six cells for the tile; rotation around the 90° angle requires four cells for the tile; and rotation around the 120° angle requires three cells for the tile. Midpoint rotation, which occurs on a single side of a shape, can be done on any shape that tessellates. If it is the only operation performed on the shape, only two cells will be required to form the tile. It should be noted that on certain shapes midpoint rotation will not always work in conjunction with other operations.

Which shapes will tessellate through rotation and which will not? As we have discovered, rotation will not work unless the shape has angles of 60°, 90°, or 120°. But not all shapes containing those angles and equal length edges at either side of those angles will tessellate by rotation. In the shape sheet shown on page 135, shapes 1, 9, and 15 have 90° angles as well as edges on either side of those 90° angles that are equal in length. Each of those shapes can be altered by rotation around the 90° corner and the result will tessellate. Shape 13 also has 90° angles as well as edges on either side of the angle that are equal in length, yet when that shape is altered with a rotation around the 90° corner, the result will not tessellate.

Shape 5 on page 135 has two angles that are 60° and two that are 120°, and all sides are equal in length. If a piece is rotated around one of the 120° angles the result will tessellate, but if it is rotated around the 60° angle it will not. Yet shapes 3 and 14 also have 60° and 120° angles, and a piece can be rotated around the 120° angle and another can be rotated around the 60° angle and

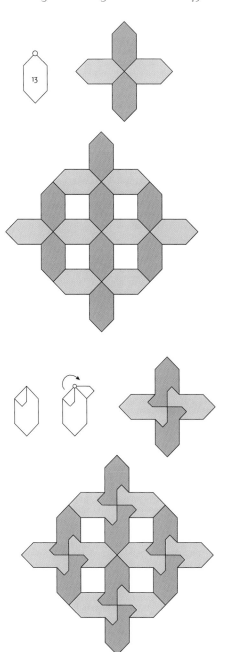

in both instances the shapes will tessellate. Why the discrepancy? Why will one shape work when the rotation is done on both angles while the other will not?

The answer, as was explained with the glide, lies in how multiples of the original shape will go together. Any time a piece is rotated around a corner, it means that three, four, or six of those shapes will have to rotate around that corner to form a tile that will repeat over and over for the design. If the original shape will not form a tile when rotated around that angle, then it also will not tessellate when a piece is cut from the shape and rotated around that same angle.

For example, a square (shape 1), a right triangle (shape 9), or the irregular pentagon (shape 15) rotated four times around a 90° corner will all form a larger tile that will translate to create a pattern. Likewise if a piece is cut out of a side of each of those shapes and rotated around the corner, and four of the resulting shapes are rotated four times around the same corner, the new tile will also form a pattern by translation, as shown with shape 15 in Illustration 7.21.

Shape 13, shown on this page, however, is different. That shape will repeat over and over by translation to form a pattern with no gaps or overlaps, but it cannot form a pattern if the shape is rotated. When four of those elongated hexagons are rotated around the 90° angle, it is apparent that the resulting shape will not repeat over and over to form a pattern. There will be gaps that would have to be filled in. Likewise if a piece is cut away from one of the sides and rotated around the 90° corner, the same thing will happen. The piece will not fit together without gaps, as shown in Illustration 7.22.

The 60° diamond (shape 5) is interesting. If that shape is rotated around the 120° angle, a hexagon is formed that will repeat over and over to form a pattern (Illustration 7.23). But if

After the shape is rotated, if there are any gaps when the pieces are put together, there will also be gaps if a piece is cut away and rotated around the same corner.

Illustration 7.22.

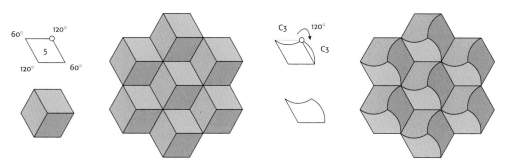

If a rotation is done around the 120° angle of the diamond, the resulting tile will tessellate. A new shape created by rotating a piece around the 120° angle will also tessellate.

Illustration 7.23.

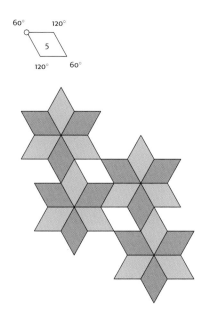

that same shape is rotated around the 60° angle, it forms a star (Illustration 7.24). The star by itself will not tessellate. Small triangles would have to be added to fill the gaps. Therefore when creating an interlocking tessellating motif from a 60° diamond, the rotation can only be done around the corners with the 120° angles.

Shapes 3 and 14 will form tiles that repeat whether they are rotated around either the 120° or the 60° angle. Therefore tessellations could be created with rotations around either of those angles.

Two examples of tessellating patterns that were created from rotations are shown on the next two pages. In *Bamboo Baskets*, the designer used a kite shape and did a rotation around the 120° angle. In *Merlin Waves His Wand*, the designer began with a square and did a rotation around the 90° angle. The photographs show the complete design and the illustrations show how the tessellated patterns were created.

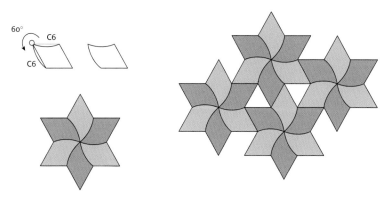

If a rotation is done around the 60° angle the resulting stars will not fill the surface without gaps. Likewise, if a piece is cut from the shape and rotated around the 60° angle, the resulting star will not tessellate.

Illustration 7.24.

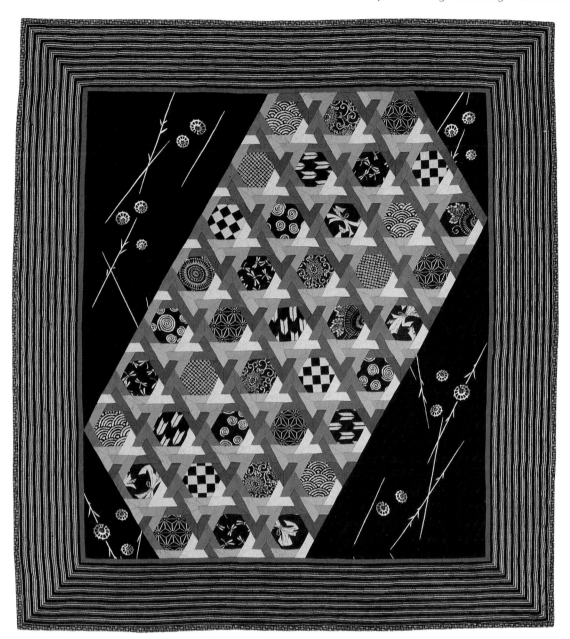

Bamboo Basket, *Yoko Sawanobori, 1995.*

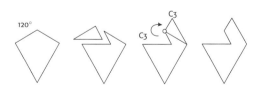

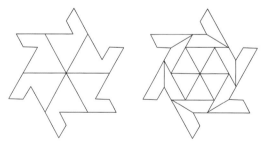

Begin with a kite shape   *Take a piece away from one side and rotate it to another around the 120° angle.*

Six of those shapes rotated form the basic pattern. Break up the inside to complete the design, and to make sewing easier.

Illustration 7.25. *Creating* Bamboo Basket.

Merlin Waves His Wand, *Kathryn Kuhn, 1996.*

    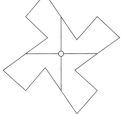 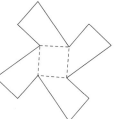

Kathryn began with a square and cut a piece out of one side and rotated it around one of the corners

Four of the shapes were rotated around the remaining right angle to obtain the tessellating shape.

The resulting shape was broken up for ease of sewing.

Illustration 7.26. Creating Merlin Waves His Wand.

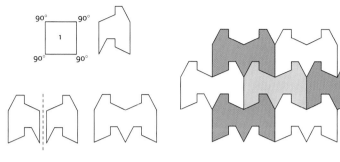

Illustration 7.27. Mirroring.

Mirror

The fourth way to alter a shape is by mirroring. In mirroring, a copy is made of the shape, and then it is flipped along an unaltered side as in Illustration 7.27. For an interlocking tessellating motif the mirror must be used with one other operation.

Not all straight sides can be mirrored and still allow the shape to tessellate. In fact a glide and a mirror in the same shape can only occur on isosceles triangles, on quadrilaterals where the glide has been done to opposite sides, and on isolated other shapes. Two mirrors cannot be performed on a shape unless the process is done along a 90° angle, and even then not all shapes with 90° angles can have two mirrors applied. When working with an equilateral triangle you cannot do a rotation around the corner and a mirror on the unaltered side, but you can do a glide from one edge to another and then mirror the unaltered side.

Knowing what will and will not work involves going to the original shape, performing the operation, and then seeing if the result tessellates. For instance, going back to page 135, shapes 2 and 3 both have 90° angles. Theoretically double mirrors could be applied to both shapes around one of the 90° angles, but when that is done, shape 2 will tessellate but shape 3, as shown in Illustration 7.28, will not.

In the case of the equilateral triangle, if a piece is rotated around one of the angles, six of the resulting shapes will form a hexagon. If the remaining side of the triangle is then mirrored, a star is formed, and, as seen earlier, that star will not tessellate without gaps. But if the piece cut from the triangle is glided instead of rotated, then the mirror can be performed on the third side. Illustration 7.29 shows the exact same piece cut from the triangle. Note that it will not tessellate if it is rotated and mirrored, but it will tessellate if it is glided and mirrored.

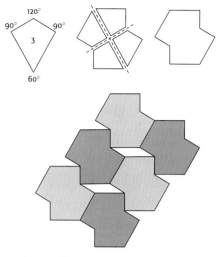

Shape 3 will not tessellate without gaps if double mirrors are applied to the 90° angle.

Illustration 7.28. Double mirrors.

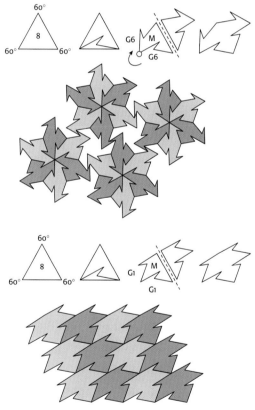

If a piece is rotated around the corner on an equilateral triangle and then the remaining side is mirrored, the result will not tessellate. But if the same piece is glided instead of rotated, a mirror can be done to the remaining side and the shape will tessellate.

Illustration 7.29. Same piece cut from a triangle.

Begin with a five-sided shape that contains a right angle and two short parallel sides.

Cut a portion of a circle out of one of the sides along the right angle, flip it, and give it back to the adjacent side of equal length.

Mirror the long side of the shape.

This pattern is an example of staggered mirror (cm) symmetry.

Illustration 7.30. Creating the Modified Clamshell *charm quilt.*

Modified Clamshell, *charm quilt, quilter unknown c. 1910.*

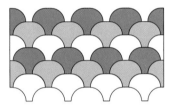

Even though it appears that this shape from Modified Spool *is the same as the one used in the* Modified Clamshell *quilt, it is not. The shapes will not fit together in this symmetry arrangement.*

Illustration 7.31.

The two antique quilts shown here both require a mirror along with another manipulation to achieve the tessellating shape. Both appear to have the same shaped piece that creates the pattern. But in fact, they are very different. One shape will not produce both designs.

The first quilt, an example of staggered mirror (cm) symmetry, is the modified clamshell. The tessellating shape for this quilt is made from the five-sided shape shown in Illustration 7.30. A piece is cut from one of the sides adjacent to the 90° angle, flipped, given back (therefore the piece is glided) to the other side adjacent to the 90° angle. The piece is then mirrored along the long side of the shape. While it appears that this shape would also produce the pattern seen in the antique quilt *Modified Spool*, you can see that it does not (Illustration 7.31).

Modified Spool, *antique charm quilt, quilter unknown, c. 1880.*

Begin with a quadrilateral with a 90° angle with two sides equal in length at either side of that angle.

Take a piece out of one of the sides adjacent to the 90° angle and rotate it around that angle.

Mirror the long side of the shape.

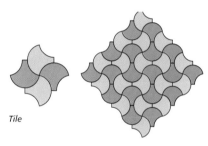

Tile

This pattern is an example of mirrored pinwheel (p4g) symmetry.

Illustration 7.32. *Creating the* **Modified Spool** *quilt.*

It is apparent that the shapes will not fit together in this pattern. A similar but different shape must be created.

Illustration 7.33.

The second antique quilt is a variation of the popular traditional quilt pattern known as *Spool, Applecore,* or *Indian Hatchet.* The pattern is mirrored pinwheel (p4g) symmetry. There is often more than one way of creating a tessellating shape and two ways to make this particular design are shown, one here (Illustration 7.32) and one on the next page. Once again you can see that even though this piece looks the same as the one in the *Modified Clamshell* quilt, subtle differences make it impossible to create the other pattern (Illustration 7.33).

The traditional *Spool* pattern combines two of the shapes into one piece, as can be seen in *Charm Quilt #480* on the next page. Creating this pattern, however, is identical to the method described in Illustration 7.32. The only difference is that the piece rotated is a slightly different curve with the narrow end

Charm Quilt #480, *Carolyn Lynch, 1990.*

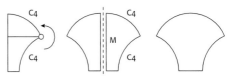

Another way to produce the same symmetry shown in Illustration 7.32 is to cut across the corner of a square into the adjacent side and rotate that piece around the corner. The unaltered side is mirrored, and the same tessellating design is produced. This shape is often used individually as in the case of the antique Modified Spool quilt, or two can be put together as one shape as in Charm Quilt #480 shown here.

This results in the same shape used in the Spool quilt.

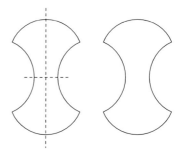

This is the shape used in Charm Quilt #480.

Illustration 7.34. Creating Charm Quilt #480.

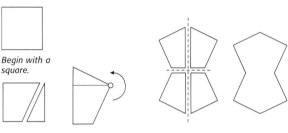

Begin with a square.

Cut a piece across the corner and rotate it.

Double mirror along the remaining right angle.

mirrored, so that the piece can be cut from one swatch of fabric (Illustration 7.34).

The pattern for the latticework in Illustration 7.35 can be created the same way as the one for the *Spool* quilt, except the only difference is that an angled piece is cut instead of a curved one.

The quilt *Infinity*, described in Illustration 7.36, is another example of the mirrored pinwheel (p4g) symmetry. The pattern is an ancient one often found in Islamic art.

Another tessellating design often found in Islamic art was used in *Cupid Misfires*, described in Illustration 7.37. The design is an example of three rotations and a mirror (p31m) symmetry. One way to create the design is shown. The original shape is an isosceles (30°, 120°, 30°) triangle (half of a 60° diamond). I find it easiest to create this design by beginning with an equilateral triangle that has been divided into three identical isosceles triangles. An underlying grid of squares also helps to get the proportions correct for the alterations, as the height of the isosceles triangle must be divided into thirds. As you can see in the illustrations, transformations made to the triangle occur both within and outside the lines of the shape. Therefore you will need to use tracing paper to make the alterations as opposed to physically cutting the piece. (See page 130.)

Once you practice with the designs in this chapter, you will find that grids are an extremely helpful tool in creating your own motifs. The precision that you can achieve from using the grid will allow more balanced, pleasing compositions that affords you greater versatility in design.

Illustration 7.35. Creating the pattern for the lattice design found at Fatepursikri, India.

Infinity, *Jennifer Heffernan, 1996. This quilt is an example of mirrored pinwheel (p4g) symmetry.*

Begin with a right-angle triangle.

Take a piece away and rotate it around the 90° angle.

Don't forget the hairline and make sure you give the piece back at the proper distance from the corner.

Mirror the long side.

Divide the design into smaller pieces for ease of sewing. Use the same fabrics in each motif.

Illustration 7.36. Creating Infinity.

Cupid Misfires, *Kathryn Kuhn, 1995.*

Use a grid that will divide the height of the isosceles triangle into thirds.

Cut a piece from one side. Note that the cut lines are parallel to the outside triangle.

Rotate around the 120° angle.

Alter the inside and outside of the isosceles triangle as shown. Since the small triangle was added to the outside of the right side of the triangle, after rotation it ends up being taken away from the left side.

Mirror the long side.

Final tessellating motif

Add lines to the shape to make it easy to sew.

Illustration 7.37. Creating Cupid Misfires.

Exercise 7
Experimenting with Tessellations

1. Working with index cards that are lined on one side, cut eight 3″ (7.5 cm) squares. Arrange them so that they all have the plain side facing up.

2. Cut a piece out of one side of one of the cards. Cut corner to corner. (This is not necessary to do, but it will make it easier to complete the exercise without getting confused.) Also to see the versatility of the design possibilities, make the cut definitely lopsided.

3. Now cut the exact same piece out of each of the other cards. Stack the cards and the cut-out pieces together.

4. Take the first card and cut-out piece and do a translation (move the piece to the opposite side that was cut). Tape the pieces together then begin at the left side and label *NTNT* clockwise around the sides of the shape.

5. Working with a tablet of paper, draw around the shape several times so that you can see how the pattern fits together. Then label that page and your shape *translation*.

6. Tape the shape to the page, and go to a new page and another one of the cut-out cards. This time do a glide straight across.

7. Continue in this fashion, and do the other two glides—one to the right, and one to the left. Label the shapes. As you draw around the shape, you will notice that every other one needs to

Step 2.

To have more versatility with this exercise, cut the piece lopsided.

Step 4.

Step 5.

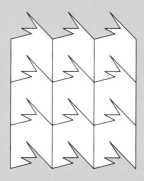

Translation

Step 6.

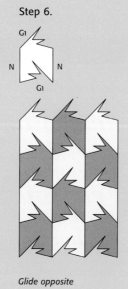

Glide opposite

Step 7.

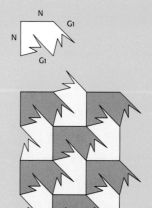

Glide right

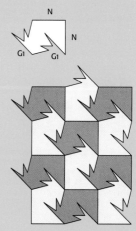

Glide left

be flipped or turned upside down. In the case of the right and left glide, in addition to being flipped, the piece will also have to be turned. As shown, the colored pieces are the ones that have been flipped. If you get confused look again at the glide examples shown here. Orient your shapes in the same direction as these. Notice that the pieces colored dark are always oriented in the same direction, and the ones colored light are always oriented the same.

8. Do a rotation around the corner with the next two cards. Rotate one to the left and one to the right. Once again label them, and draw around them a few times. This time the pieces will not be flipped but will simply be rotated to fit together. It will be easiest to fit them together if you rotate them around the same corner that you rotated the piece. For later reference be sure to label each piece.

9. Take the last two cards, and translate them as you did with the first card. Now orient them in the same direction, and stack them on top of each other. Take the top card and open it just as you would open a book, and tape the two edges together. Draw around the shape, and label it *mirror*.

Step 8.

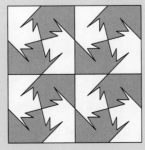

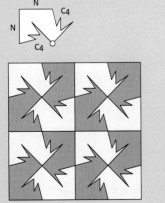

Rotate right   *Rotate left*

Step 9.

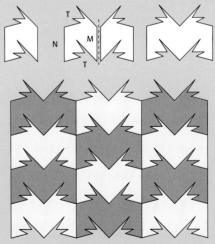

Mirror

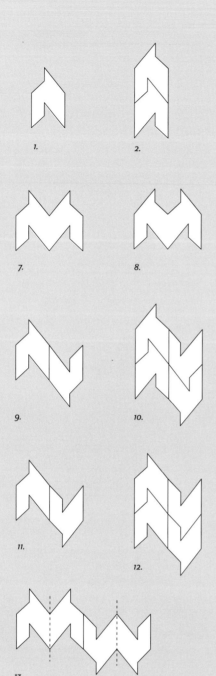

Applying Symmetries

The following list corresponds to the patterns shown on page 5, and the tiles that make up those patterns are shown here with explanations of the operations performed to achieve the designs. The first seven are exactly as in Exercise 7. The remaining ones had various symmetries applied to them. The illustrations show the tiles that repeat for each of the patterns.

1. The piece that was taken away was translated to the opposite side, and the tile was translated for the design.
2. The piece was glided to the opposite side (flipped horizontally and moved to the parallel side).
3. The piece was glided to the right side of the square.
4. The piece was glided to the left side of the square.
5. A rotation was made to the right side of the square.
6. A rotation was made to the left side of the square.
7. The translation that was done in number 1 has now been mirrored.
8. The glide that was done in number 2 has been mirrored.

The next three are very similar in look, but there are subtle differences.

9. The piece was translated, and a midpoint rotation (p2) was done to put the units together.
10. This one is the same as number 9 except that the piece was glided to the opposite side, and then the units were put together with midpoint rotation (p2). Four cells are necessary to create the tile.
11. The piece was translated, but this time the next shape was glided (moved sideways and flipped upside down).

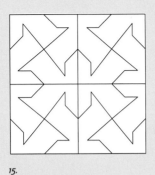
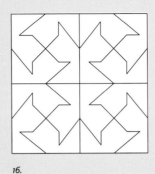
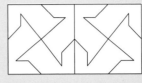
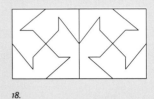

15.

16.

17.

18.

12. This time the piece was glided and the next unit was also glided to create the tile.

13. The translated unit has been mirrored, and then the mirrored pair has been flipped upside down.

14. The glided unit has been mirrored, and the mirrored pair has been flipped upside down.

15. This is the mirrored pinwheel (p4g) symmetry. The piece that was cut was rotated around the right corner, and four of them were put together to create the pinwheel unit. Then that unit was mirrored on all sides.

16. This is the same as number 15 except the cutout piece was rotated to the left instead of to the right.

The last four patterns apply some of the symmetries to the rotated units in numbers 5 and 6.

17. The rotated unit from number 5 has been mirrored.

18. The rotated unit from number 6 has been mirrored.

19. The rotated unit from number 5 has been double mirrored and then those double mirror units have been staggered.

20. This is the same as number 19 except that the rotated unit is from number 6.

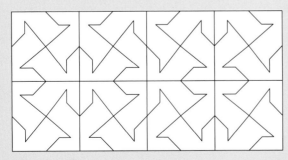
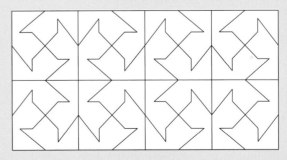

19.

20.

1. Translate   2. Glide opposite   3. Glide left   4. Glide right   5. Rotate right   6. Rotate left

Illustration 7.38a. How might you next change the unaltered sides of these six shapes?

Combining Operations

In creating tessellations every side of a shape that tessellates can be altered, and combinations of the different operations can produce many different designs, all of which fall into one of the symmetry groups. Before looking into physically altering other sides of the shape, however, lets look at the design options of just applying the symmetries to the shapes you have already created in Exercise 4.

In the exercise only two sides of the square were altered and that produced seven different patterns. In actual fact many more patterns can be created with that single piece cut from a square. In the discussion on symmetry on page 6 it was noted that a square primary cell can be used to create patterns in 11 of the 17 two-dimensional symmetries, and since more than one pattern can be made with some of the symmetries, there are 24 total possible patterns that can be created. Those same symmetry operations can also be used on the "interlocking" tessellated square to create additional patterns.

Look again at the 20 designs on page 5. Each of them was created with just a single piece being cut from a square. The piece was given back by translation, glide, and rotation; then various symmetries were applied to create the patterns. Study the designs on those pages and see if you can figure out what was done to create each one. After you have studied them, check with the list on pages 158–159 and see how many you were able to decipher.

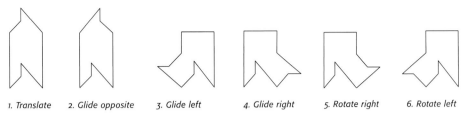

1. Translate   2. Glide opposite   3. Glide left   4. Glide right   5. Rotate right   6. Rotate left

Illustration 7.38b. How might you next change the unaltered sides of these six shapes?

You have seen how many different designs can be created from taking only a single piece out of a square and giving it back in a variety of ways. Even more options open up when you alter one or more of the remaining sides of the shape. For example the six cells that were created from a square to form the designs on page 5 are numbered and shown in Illustration 7.38. In the second set of illustrations, the same operations are performed on a rectangle. Look at each one and think about what could be done to it to alter the remaining sides. There are scores of possibilities and space precludes showing all of the options here, therefore only the first cell that was used will be shown. Once you see the possibilities for that one cell, you can imagine how many others there are with the other cells. Experiment with some of the options with the pieces you created in Exercise 4.

In Illustration 7.39 cell number 1 is used and the same shaped piece has been cut from a portion of one of the remaining unaltered sides. The piece can be moved in four different ways. It can be translated or glided to the opposite side or it can be midpoint rotated on that same side. If it is midpoint rotated there is still one remaining unaltered side and that can be changed as well by either another midpoint rotation or a mirror. The designs can also look very different depending on which side the piece is taken from. The first four illustrations have the piece taken from the left side of the shape, whereas the next four have the same piece taken from the right side.

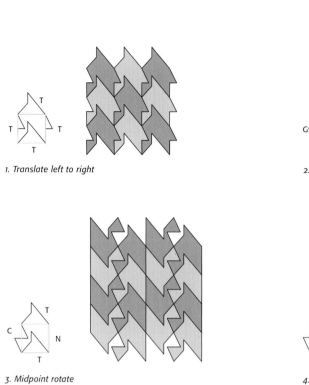

1. Translate left to right

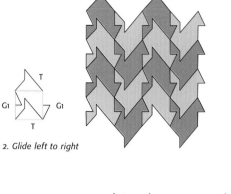

2. Glide left to right

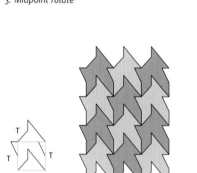

3. Midpoint rotate

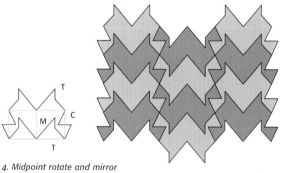

4. Midpoint rotate and mirror

5. Translate right to left

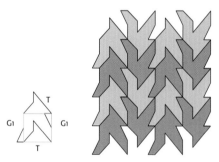

6. Glide right to left

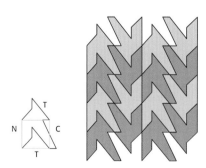

7. Midpoint rotate right side

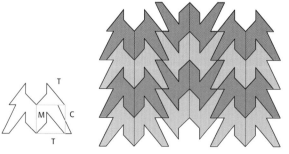

8. Midpoint rotate right side and mirror left side

Illustration 7.39. Combining operations, beginning with a square that has been altered with translation from bottom to top. Another cut has been taken from one of the other remaining unaltered sides. Even through that second alteration is the same in all examples, totally different patterns emerge depending on which side the cut was made and what operation was performed.

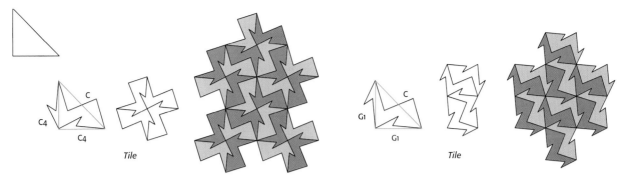

The same piece has been cut from the side of the triangle. The one on the left has been rotated around the corner, and the one on the right has been glided. Both triangles have the same shape midpoint rotated on the long side of the triangle.

Illustration 7.40. Combining operations, beginning with an isosceles triangle.

When working with isosceles triangles (ones in which at least two sides are equal in length) there are only two operations that can be performed on the two equal sides, a glide and a rotation. Note that any isosceles triangle can have a glide performed on the two equal sides, but not every isosceles triangle can have a rotation applied to those sides. Whether or not a rotation can be done depends on the angle around which the rotation will occur. As noted earlier, it must be an angle of 60°, 90°, or 120°. The remaining side can always be midpoint rotated, and if a glide was performed it can always be mirrored. If a rotation occurred, it can sometimes be mirrored and sometimes not, depending on the specific triangle.

The pattern created from an altered triangle can look completely different depending on whether the two equal sides are rotated or glided. In Illustration 7.40, the same pieces have been cut from an isosceles triangle. The one on the left has been rotated, and the one on the right has been glided. The third side has been midpoint rotated in both with the same cut. The patterns that are created look very different from each one and serve as another reminder of all the options you have when experimenting with tessellations.

When you are working with a hexagon, after two or three of the sides have been altered it can become confusing as to which sides have been changed and which have not. I usually like to label the sides before I start. For example, if I want to translate all sides of a hexagon, I will label opposite sides with the same number or letter. As I translate each of the sides to an opposite and parallel side, I move the *o* side to the other *o* side, the *x* to the opposite *x*, etc. Illustration 7.41 shows how confusing it could become if the sides were not labeled.

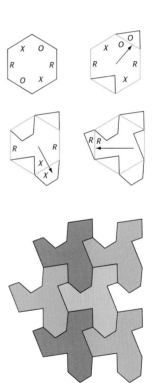

Illustration 7.41. Combining operations, beginning with a hexagon.

A Note to Quilters

When I teach workshops on tessellations to groups of quilters I find that participants immediately want to know how the designs they create can be adapted to quilt making. While I prefer teaching the design process first, I find quilters cannot get this out of their minds. My guess is that many people reading this book will feel the same way, so a brief explanation is given here and more will follow in later chapters.

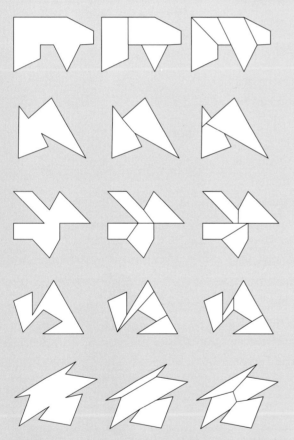

Dividing a shape for easy sewing. Here are two different ways each of five shapes can be broken up for piecing.

The tessellations you make will first be developed on small index cards or on tracing paper before you transfer them to fabric. Remember that if the design you create is to be made into a quilt, you will be working with a much larger unit than the one in which the design was created. First, decide how large you would like the motif to be and re-create the design to that size. Second, if you want to think about creating a design for quilting, keep curves gentle and avoid sharp angles.

Once you are satisfied with the design, the next step is to determine how it will be sewn. Keep in mind that any time there is an inward angle, a seam will need to go to that angle. Therefore, the shape will have to be broken down into smaller pieces, depending on how many inward angles there are. If you wish, you can still use the same fabric for all pieces in the shape. Some of the tessellating shapes used in this chapter are illustrated on this page. In each case, two different ways that they could be broken up for piecing are given. The next few chapters will provide more information on using tessellations in quilt making, but this should at least answer some of the initial questions.

1. Translate.

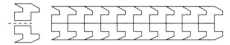

2. Translate and mirror the bottom edge.

Illustration 7.42. Fifteen borders created from a square.

Tessellating Borders

Once you understand the basics of creating interlocking motifs, creating borders that tessellate is very easy. Chapter 5 discussed the linear symmetries and how to achieve them. The same processes can be done for the interlocking border designs. The main consideration is to have two parallel straight sides for the finished strip of border. Therefore it is only possible to glide to the opposite side of the piece. If it is glided to one of the sides, there will be no possibility for two straight and parallel edges.

Illustration 7.42 shows the 15 different borders that can be created when one piece is cut from the side of a square and given back to one of the other sides.

Endless Design Possibilities

As you can see, the possibilities for design are endless. The only problem is in finding the time to experiment. While guidelines have been given throughout this text to help you determine which shapes can have which types of alterations, the shape sheet you first saw on page 135 is presented opposite, complete with symmetry operations as a quick reference to help you immediately begin working with several common shapes. The transformations that can be done to each shape are listed according to the labeling system described, here and on page 128.

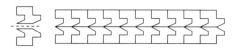

3. Translate and mirror the top edge.

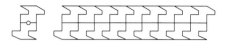

4. Translate and midpoint rotate the bottom edge.

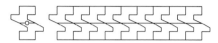

5. Translate and midpoint rotate the top edge.

6. Rotate to the top.

7. Rotate to the bottom.

8. Glide.

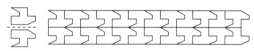

9. Glide and mirror.

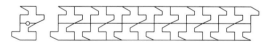

10. Glide and midpoint rotate.

11. Midpoint rotate.

12. Midpoint rotate and mirror the side.

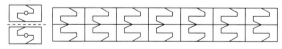

13. Midpoint rotate and mirror the top or bottom.

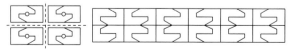

14. Midpoint rotate and mirror the side and the top or bottom.

15. Midpoint rotate the side and either the top or bottom.

Rhapsody, *Jinny Beyer, 1997.*
The pattern of this quilt is an example of six rotation (p6) symmetry. The tessellating motif was created from an equilateral triangle by means of rotation.

CHAPTER 8

Refining Tessellations: *Shape and Color*

IF YOU ARE A QUILTER, STAINED-GLASS ARTIST, woodworker, or artist who works in some other medium that involves cutting pieces apart and putting them back together again, you may wonder how all of the interlocking designs that were created from index cards as in Chapter 7 can be applied to your work. The purpose of working with index cards was to help you become familiar with tessellations and to experiment with all of the techniques for making them. In this chapter you will see how easy it is to apply those techniques to patterns that you would like to create in your field of design.

Illustration 8.1. How might you approach recreating this fabric for your own medium?

Preparing Tessellations for Construction in Surface Design

As you look at your collection of index-card designs created in the previous chapter, it may be difficult to see how these will translate into your own medium. For instance, there may be curves that are too deep, angles that are too sharp, or too many points meeting at one place. First, remember that you will most likely be working with a much larger unit than the 3″ (7.5 cm) square that was used in Chapter 7. Second, when you begin to design a motif do not lose sight of your medium. As you alter the sides of your shape, think about how difficult it might be to reconstruct the motif in your desired medium. It is wise when working in fabric, for example, to keep sharp angles at a minimum and to make the curves gentle.

Rhapsody (shown on page 166) was developed from a small triangle cut from an index card. I smoothed out some of the deeper curves and thought about how large the unit should be. Finally I redrew the design beginning with an equilateral triangle that was 12″ (30 cm) per side. Even though the curves appeared as though they would be hard to sew in the small version, once the larger version was made, the curves were much gentler and not at all difficult to construct.

If the tessellated design has only gentle curves, it is possible that it can be cut out all in one piece from the same fabric, glass, wood, or paper. Examples of patterns that would work are the quilt patterns *Modified Clamshell* and *Modified Spool*, seen on pages 150 and 151. If the design has angles, however, the shape must be broken down into two or more pieces, depending on how many inward angles there are. In other words, for construction purposes, any time there is an inward angle, there must be a joining point or seam going to that angle.

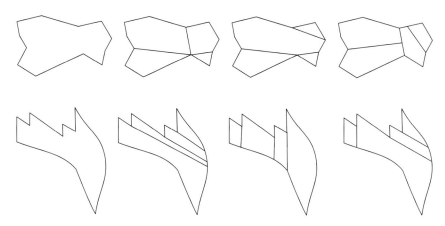

There are many ways to break up a shape for construction. Illustration 8.2 demonstrates multiple ways of breaking up two simple shapes for entirely different effects. For ease of construction, each has been broken up into as few segments as possible.

Even if you have to break a design into two or more pieces for construction purposes, you can still use the same material for all pieces within each individual unit. For design purposes, however, you may prefer to use different fabrics, glass, or wood. As you will see, you may also choose subtle variations of the same color. You will find that sometimes changes like these help accentuate the tessellation or send it into relief. Whatever you use, make sure that there is enough contrast from one unit to the next so that the original shape is apparent in the overall design.

Illustration 8.2. Breaking up shapes.

Preparing Tessellations for Color and Value

Another way to divide a shape that will make it easier to construct and also create some very interesting design effects is to break it into bands that can later be shaded with color values.

There are many ways to create these bands. I like to draw around the shape, imagine a focal point outside of the design itself, and then draw lines across the shape to that focal point. This creates tapered bands, which I find more aesthetically pleasing than straight bands. (See Illustration 8.3.) Illustration 8.4 demonstrates this technique. If the focal point is made on the design itself, there will be too many points coming together at the same place. This would make the design difficult to construct. If you are planning to construct the design in fabric, it is important to remember the inward-angle rule and to have lines coming

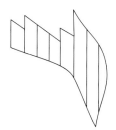

Illustration 8.3. Breaking up shapes for construction. It is more interesting from a design standpoint for the bands to be tapered, top, as opposed to being straight, bottom.

Value Differences in Interlocking Shapes

For the individual shapes within a repeating design to stand out there must be differences in value among the pieces. When tessellations are made from squares or rectangles, only two values of coloring are needed for the individual motifs to stand out. When a hexagon is used, however, three different values are needed for the individual motifs to be distinguishable.

When a shape with a 120° angle is used to create the tessellation, if it is translated only two values are needed, but if it is rotated around the 120° angle three values are needed. Other shapes, depending on the layouts used or the cuts made to create the designs, might also need light, medium, and dark values within the various pieces.

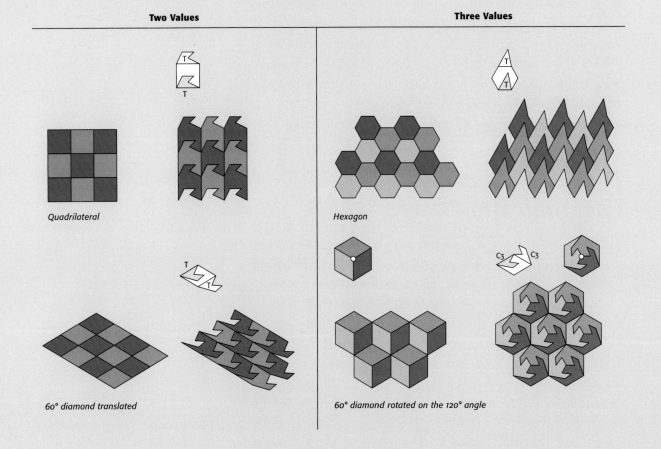

Two Values

Quadrilateral

60° diamond translated

Three Values

Hexagon

60° diamond rotated on the 120° angle

from or going through those angles to the focal point. Experiment with several different focal points. You never know which one will give the most interest when several of the completed motifs are joined together. The same designs used in Illustration 8.2 to show how to break up a design for construction purposes have been used again to show how to create tapered bands (Illustration 8.4). Notice how different the three variations are.

Coloring the Design

Once the design is broken into bands, the easiest way to introduce color is to begin by simply shading the unit from light to dark, or with subtle shading differences within the units. I usually try several different ways of shading the unit to see which variation seems best. It is only then that I decide on a color palette and execute the design in fabric. The palette of colors will contain fabrics that are shaded from light to dark. I follow the same light to dark shading in color that was done in black and white, and I make the colors in each unit a little different, while still maintaining the same shading guide. Illustration 8.5 shows how the same unit can look depending on how it is shaded.

As explained earlier, if each unit is all one color, there must be value differences between the units for them to show up in the overall pattern. If the tessellating unit is being broken into bands this does not necessarily have to be done, as you have seen. In fact I think that it is often more interesting if the units are shaded with different hues of more or less the same values. Depending on how the shading was done, the units will still stand out or perhaps create other interesting designs, as can be seen in the quilts shown on pages 174–177.

Designing for Your Medium

If you are a quilter wanting to create a design in fabric, you will need to look at the process a little differently than a graphic artist working on paper or canvas. That is because quilters have to keep in mind the logistics of cutting and sewing together pieces of fabric. The angles must be less sharp and the curves gentle.

Note that in any medium, where pieces have been cut out and then rejoined, if a mirror or a glide was used in the design, half of the units need to be reversed (mirror imaged) from the other half.

Shape 1, variation 1

Shape 1, variation 2

Shape 1, variation 3

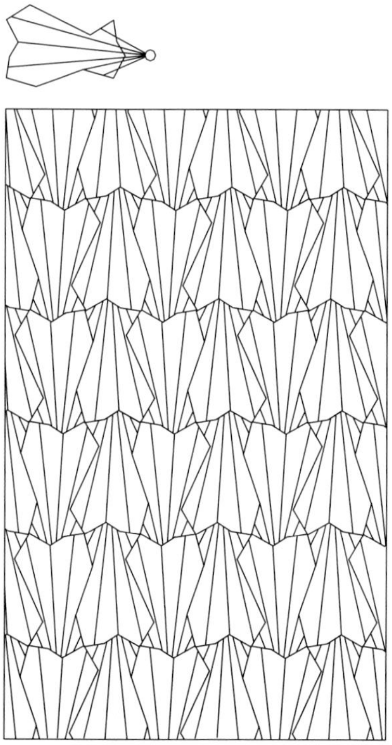

Shape 2, variation 1

Shape 2, variation 2

Shape 2, variation 3

Illustration 8.4. Experimenting with shapes. The same two shapes used in Illustration 8.3 are now broken up using focal points outside the design, as indicated by the dots.

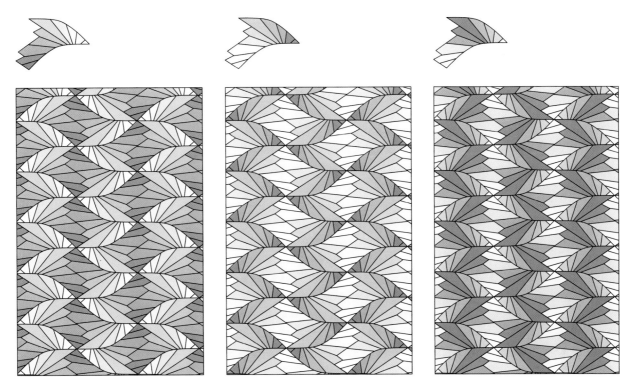

Illustration 8.5. The effects of shading. The same unit, shaded three ways, results in a very different look.

Experiments in Value

The tessellating shape in Illustration 8.5 is the one I used for my quilt *Soaring High* (Illustration 8.6). I worked with shaded bands of color but alternated between dark and light units so that the individual tessellated shapes would stand out. There are so many options for creating the coloring within the tessellating motifs that you just have to experiment and come up with the option you like best.

The technique of working with shaded bands of colors was used in three other quilts shown in this book. The quilt *Wild One* is created from a square, with pieces rotated around two corners to create the motif. (See Illustration 8.7.) The designer then created a focal point off the motif and drew lines to that focal point. She made sure that one of the lines went through the inward angle so that it would be easy to sew. The unit was then shaded several times and photocopied. Once she was satisfied with the way the units looked, she created her palette of colors and cut and sewed the pieces together following the light-to-dark shading that was done in black and white. Because of the use of color, a secondary pinwheel design becomes the focus of the pattern.

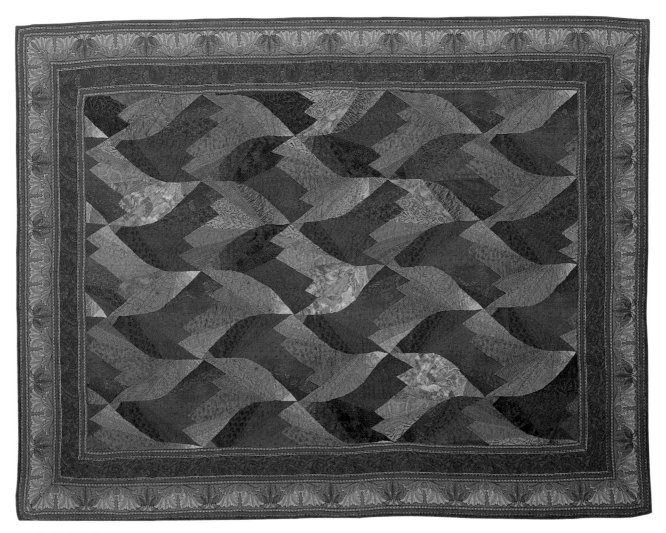

Soaring High, *Jinny Beyer, 1998.*

   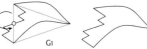

*Begin with an
isosceles
triangle.*

*Glide a piece from one of the long
sides to the other long side.*

Midpoint rotate the short side.

*Draw bands for
shading, making sure
that lines go to all of
the inward angles.*

*Because there was a glide
involved in the designing,
half of the pieces will
have to be reversed.*

*Illustration 8.6. Creating Soaring High. See other design options for this
tessellating motif on page 172.*

Wild One, Yoko Sawanobori, 1993.

| Begin with a square. | Cut a piece out of one side. | Rotate it around the corner. | Cut a piece from one of the remaining sides. | Rotate it around the corner. | Completed shape | Create a focal point and draw lines to the point. | Completed shaded design | Unit of four rotated motifs repeats 20 times. |

Illustration 8.7. Creating Wild One.

Detail of Rhapsody, *Jinny Beyer. (See page 166.)*

Begin with an equilateral triangle.

Take part of a circle out of one side.

Rotate it around the corner to an adjacent side.

Take a partial circle out of half of the unaltered side.

Midpoint rotate it to the other half of the side.

Completed shape

Create a focal point and draw bands to use for color shading.

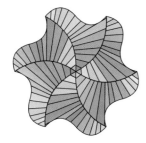

Tile made up of six primary cells or units that was used in the quilt Rhapsody

Illustration 8.8. Creating Rhapsody.

When designing the quilt *Rhapsody*, which is shown on page 166, I began with an equilateral triangle. A curved piece was cut out of one side and rotated around the corner to an adjacent side. The third side was midpoint rotated as in Illustration 8.8. I then created a focal point off of the motif and drew straight lines to that point. Each band represented a different pattern piece. Rather than shade from light to dark in exactly the same way on each unit, I chose to subtly shade from one color to the next. Sometimes the darkest fabrics were in the middle of the unit and sometimes they were at one of the ends. The individual units were very easy to sew because the pieces were all straight. However, sewing the units together was a little more difficult because of the curves. But because the pieces were so large—I began with an equilateral triangle that was 12″ (30 cm) per side—the curves were not as difficult to sew as one might think.

Normally when all of the blocks or units for a design are complete I like to pin them to a wall and work with the arrangement until I am satisfied with the placement. The pieces for this quilt were so oddly shaped that it was difficult to get them to pin neatly next to each other. I finally opted to create a larger unit or tile made up of six of the smaller motifs. The six pieces rotated around the 60° angle to form the tile, which makes this quilt the six rotation or p6 symmetry. Within each tile I strived to create a diversity of color and pattern as I placed the motifs. Then when the tiles were complete, it was easier to pin them to the wall and achieve an overall color balance than it was to work with the individual cells.

A kite shape, six of which form a hexagonal tile, was the piece I began with to design *Day Lilies* (Illustration 8.9). A c3 rotation was done around the 120° angle, and a c6 rotation was done around the 60° angle. I placed a focal point outside of the shape and drew straight lines to that point, making sure that a seam cut through any inward angles.

Day Lilies, *Jinny Beyer, 1998.*

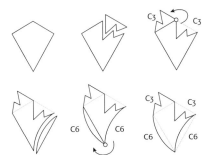

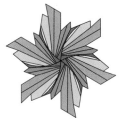

Create a focal point
and draw bands to
use for color shading.

Shaded unit

Six units form the completed tile.

Illustration 8.9. Creating Day Lilies.

Finishing Off the Design

One of the first questions asked after a novice designer draws around a tessellating motif several times and views the ragged edge, is "How do I finish off the pattern?" While some people like to finish their design with an irregular edge, others like to square it off. I, too, like to even out the edges.

1. When putting triangles together, there is an uneven edge unless half triangles are used to fill in the gaps.

One of the easiest ways to straighten the edges is to go back to the underlying grid and then fill in with partial shapes. For instance in *Rhapsody*, shown in Illustration 8.8, the original shape was an equilateral triangle. If multiple triangles are put together, the result will be an irregular edge at the sides. In order to square it off, half triangles would have to be inserted to fill the gaps, as illustrated above. Once the interlocking design has been created, that underlying grid of triangles still exists, as illustrated on the left. Therefore you can still fill in with half triangles, but this time they will be in the form of the pattern.

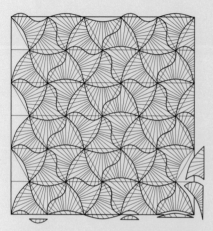

2. When working with a tessellating motif that has an underlying of triangles, partial shapes will also have to be used to fill in the half triangle gaps.

If you are making a quilt, as opposed to drawing your design onto a surface, you will discover that straightening out the edges in this manner produces many small pieces that would require separate templates. For a simpler way to create squared edging, try the following method.

Make large pattern pieces of the size required to fill in the various places. Then, work with full units that are already sewn and cut the fill-in pieces from those sewn motifs, as can be seen on the bottom and right edges of the second illustration. Sometimes you can use two different parts of the same motif. After cutting, go back and reinforce the seams.

The edges on the *Day Lilies* quilt were also straightened out in a similar manner. Working with units that had already been sewn, I cut the necessary pieces for filling in the edges, making sure to add seam allowances on all pieces.

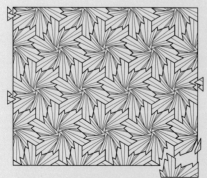

3. Edging for Day Lilies *(page 177).*

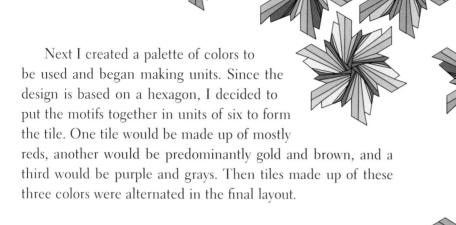

Next I created a palette of colors to be used and began making units. Since the design is based on a hexagon, I decided to put the motifs together in units of six to form the tile. One tile would be made up of mostly reds, another would be predominantly gold and brown, and a third would be purple and grays. Then tiles made up of these three colors were alternated in the final layout.

Design Options for All Media

The ideas presented in this chapter are meant to inspire you to try similar experiments in whatever artistic medium you choose. Quilts have been emphasized here mainly because I work with quilts and have experimented with these techniques with students. Some of these tessellation concepts have been applied to knitting patterns I have designed, and I would love to see some of the same ideas applied to mosaic wood designs, stained glass, and other areas of artistic endeavor. Once you feel comfortable creating tessellations you will be amazed at how many design options unfold.

Water Lily, *Jinny Beyer, 1986.*
Two different patchwork blocks, both examples of traditional block (p4m)
symmetry, were alternated to create the pattern for this quilt. The pieced
border is an example of vertical mirror (m1) symmetry.

CHAPTER 9

Creating *Geometric* Tessellations

TILE FLOORS, MOSAIC WALLS, TESSELLATING
borders, and interlocking patchwork designs have
always intrigued me. From ancient times, tessellating motifs have been used to create geometric
surface designs. While the representational images
of Escher amaze me, it is the more traditional
interlocking geometric designs that appeal to me
the most. It has been my desire to create these
types of patterns that has fueled my interest in
tessellations. Experimentation, beginning with
the most simple of shapes, led to many discoveries,
which I will share in this chapter. We will explore
not only how to make tessellations by applying
the symmetries to a variety of shapes, but also
how the addition of value and contrast adds an
entirely new dimension to geometric patterns.

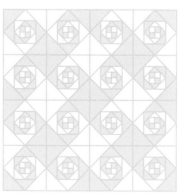

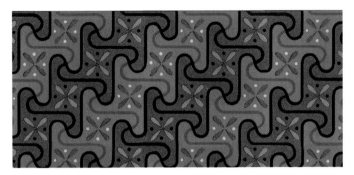

Illustration 9.1. Tessellating architectural ornamentation from ancient Egypt.

Tessellations for All Surface Designers

Since much of my design work has dealt with patchwork and quilting, I first looked at tessellations through the eyes of a quilter. I soon found that the techniques I discovered were an invaluable lesson to me in the design of printed fabric. In fact, the principles that govern the creation of tessellations apply to all areas of surface design. From the intricate mosaic tile designs in the Alhambra, Spain, that so intrigued M. C. Escher to contemporary artistry in glass, textiles, and graphic design, tessellations are everywhere.

Two methods of creating traditional, geometric tessellations will be discussed here. The first method is developing the designs from individual shapes, and the second is developing tessellation motifs from existing traditional patterns.

Creating Geometric Tessellations from Simple Shapes

To create geometric tessellations that are completely square, you must start with a square, rectangle, or right (half-square) triangle. The trick is to leave two sides unaltered, so that when multiples of the cells you make come together, they always form a perfect square. Changes can only be made to a single side or to two sides that are adjacent to each other. And these alterations, like the shapes they are made to, must be angular and geometric. Taking a curved segment out of a square will not yield the type of geometric designs we discuss in this chapter.

Working with any underlying grid will make it easier to get the angles and lines even, and will help you make the alterations proportional to the shape. The grid will also provide a guide to re-create the design in a larger size.

Working with an underlying grid, cut a piece out of one side of a square.

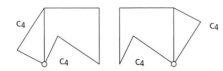

Rotate it around one of the corners (to left or right).

 or

Rotate four of these modified squares around the same corner that the original rotation took place.

 *or*

Color alternate squares dark and light.

Illustration 9.2. Rotation around a corner to create a square tile.

Working with a Square

There are only two operations that can be performed on a square that will give you a resulting tile that is also a square. The first is a rotation around one of the corners, and the second is a midpoint rotation on one of the sides.

Rotation Around the Corner

First, cut a piece from a side of a square and rotate it around one of the corners. Then rotate four of the resulting motifs around that same corner to form a larger square. At this point, the tile can either be left as a line drawing or alternating cells can be colored dark and light. Try it both ways to see the different effects.

Next this tile can be treated as though it is a primary cell and all of the various symmetries can be applied to result in several additional tessellating designs. Since the tile is made up of four cells that have rotational symmetry, there are not as many pattern possibilities as there would be if there were no repeating parts. Many of the symmetries will give the same results. Several of the pattern possibilities are shown in Illustration 9.3. Translation (p1), midpoint rotation (p2), and pinwheel rotation (p4) all result in the same pattern (1). Mirror (pm), glide (pg), and glided staggered mirror (pmg) all create a second pattern (2). And, in the same way, double mirror (pmm), double glide (pgg), mirrored pinwheel (p4g), and staggered mirror (cm) all result in a third pattern (3).

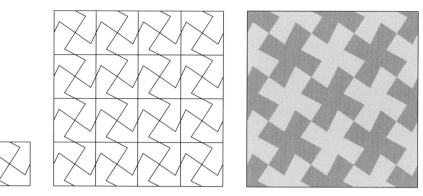

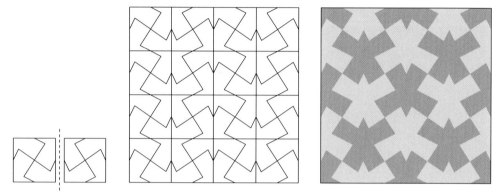

1. Translation (p1), midpoint rotation (p2), and pinwheel (p4) all produce the same pattern.

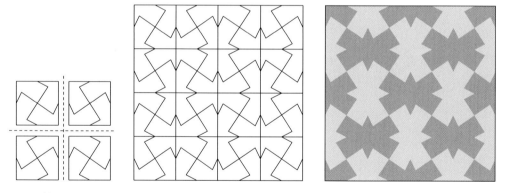

2. Mirror (pm), glide (pg), and glided staggered mirror (pmg) all result in the same pattern.

3. Double mirror (pmm), double glide (pgg), mirrored pinwheel (p4g), and staggered mirror (cm) all result in the same pattern.

Illustration 9.3. Six patterns from the same rotated unit.

The first three patterns all produce single tessellating motifs, but the next three are particularly interesting in that they create two or more motifs that interlock perfectly. The staggered double mirror symmetry (cmm) produced the fourth pattern that combines the two motifs found in patterns (2) and (3). The fifth pattern also contains two different motifs, one that appears in (2)

4. *Staggered double mirror (cmm)*

5. *This pattern is formed **by taking four of the rotated units and mirroring them (pm) to create the repeating tile.***

6. *This pattern is formed by taking four of the rotated units and double-mirroring them (pmm) to create the repeating tile.*

and the other that appears in (1). To arrive at this design, four of the rotated squares are mirrored. The sixth pattern contains three tessellating motifs, the first from pattern (1), the second from pattern (2) and the third from pattern (3).

As you can see, when working with one simple alteration of a square, a wide variety of patterns emerges.

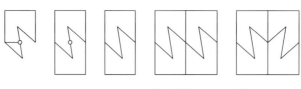

Translation   Mirror

Illustration 9.4. Remaking a square tile through midpoint rotation.

Square made from a mirrored rectangle

Midpoint Rotation on One Side

Midpoint rotation is the second operation that will result in a tessellating tile that is a square. First, a simple midpoint rotation to one of the sides of the square will result in a rectangular motif. To get back to a square, that shape must be either mirrored or translated (Illustration 9.4). Various symmetries can then be applied to that tile. I find that with this method the most interesting tessellations are achieved by applying the pinwheel (p4) symmetry to either of the tiles (Illustration 9.5).

Working with a Rectangle

The only operation that can be done to a rectangle to result in a square tile is midpoint rotation on one of the long sides. The rectangle must be twice as long as it is wide. Once that is done, and the two sections are colored light and dark, nine of the eleven symmetries can be applied for a total of five different one-motif patterns. Since there is symmetry within the square, some of the symmetry operations produce the same pattern. Some of the patterns produce more traditional designs than others. The five one-motif patterns, along with several patterns shaded with different color values are shown in Illustrations 9.6 and 9.7, first as line drawings, and then once the cells have been colored. It should be noted that staggered double mirror (cmm) and mirrored pinwheel (p4g) create designs with more than one tessellating motif.

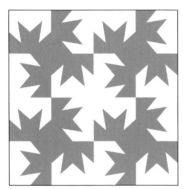

Square made from a translated rectangle

Illustration 9.5. Pinwheel (p4) symmetry applied to square tile.

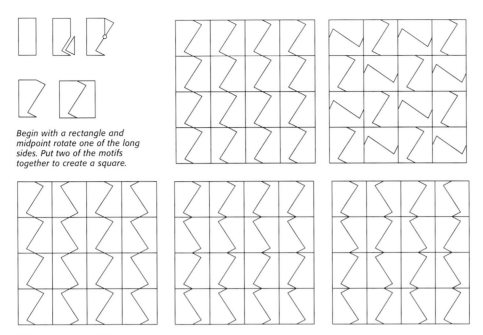

Begin with a rectangle and midpoint rotate one of the long sides. Put two of the motifs together to create a square.

Illustration 9.6. Five patterns created by applying symmetries to a square formed by midpoint rotation to a rectangle.

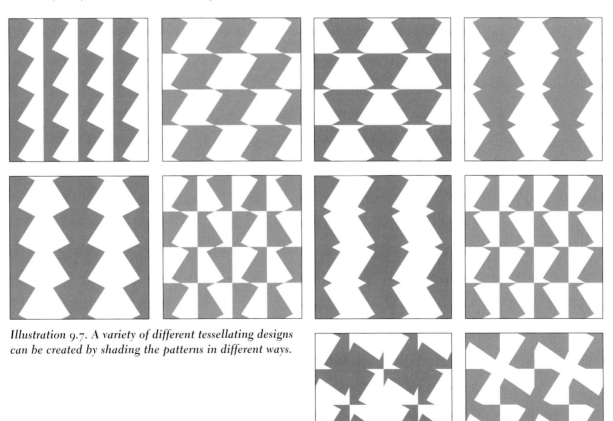

Illustration 9.7. A variety of different tessellating designs can be created by shading the patterns in different ways.

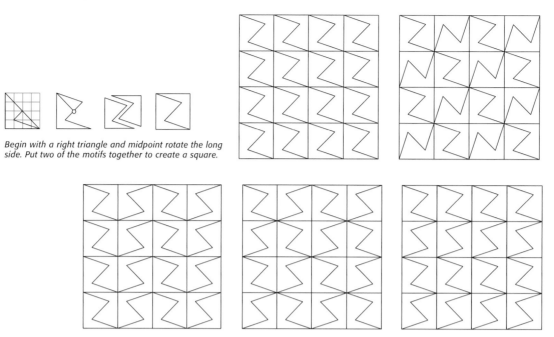

Begin with a right triangle and midpoint rotate the long side. Put two of the motifs together to create a square.

Illustration 9.8. Five patterns created by applying symmetries to a right (half-square) triangle.

Working with a Right Triangle

A right triangle (or half-square triangle) can also be used to create geometric tessellating motifs that form a square tile. The triangle can be altered in two different ways: first, with a midpoint rotation along the long side and second with a c4 rotation around the 90° angle.

Midpoint Rotation

A piece is cut from the long side of the triangle and midpoint rotated to the other side. Two of the resulting motifs are joined together to form a square; one is colored light and the other dark. Next all of the 11 symmetries that can be applied to a square can be applied to this tile to create several designs (Illustration 9.6 and 9.7).

Illustrations 9.8 and 9.9 show how a right triangle with a midpoint rotation on the long side can produce traditional geometric tessellating motifs. Thus, five patterns can be created using 9 of the 11 symmetries that apply to a square created from a right triangle. These will all produce single tessellating motifs. The other two symmetries, mirrored pinwheel (p4g) and staggered mirror (cmm) produce patterns with more than one tessellating shape.

Illustration 9.9. A variety of different tessellating designs can be created by shading the patterns in different ways.

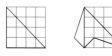

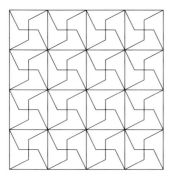

Begin with a right-angle triangle, but this time instead of a midpoint rotation, rotate the piece around the 90° angle. Then rotate four of those around the same angle.

Coloring the tile two different ways will yield a variety of tessellating designs

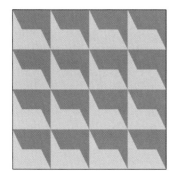

Translation (p1) and midpoint rotation (p2)

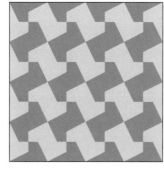

Translation (p1)

Rotation Around the 90° Angle

The second method of creating geometric tessellating motifs from a right triangle is to do a rotation around the 90° angle. Nine of the symmetries produce four different patterns when just viewed as line drawings. However, when the tile is colored in just two different ways and the symmetries applied again, you can see how different the patterns look. The three colored examples with each of the line drawings in Illustrations 9.10 and 9.11 have the same underlying design. Adding color value has just changed the way they look.

Translation (p1)

Midpoint rotation (p2)

Illustration 9.10. Applying different operations to the shaded tiles creates a variety of designs.

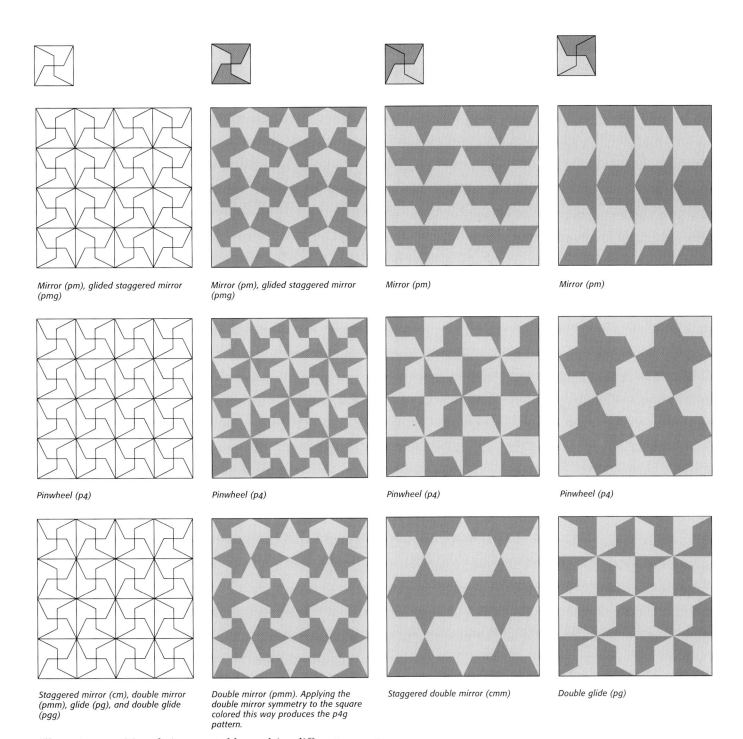

Mirror (pm), glided staggered mirror (pmg)

Mirror (pm), glided staggered mirror (pmg)

Mirror (pm)

Mirror (pm)

Pinwheel (p4)

Pinwheel (p4)

Pinwheel (p4)

Pinwheel (p4)

Staggered mirror (cm), double mirror (pmm), glide (pg), and double glide (pgg)

Double mirror (pmm). Applying the double mirror symmetry to the square colored this way produces the p4g pattern.

Staggered double mirror (cmm)

Double glide (pg)

Illustration 9.11. More designs created by applying different symmetry operations to the shaded tile created from the right triangle.

Illustration 9.12. Line drawing of design used for the Virginia Reel *pattern and a traditional value-shading of the design.*

The Miraculous Effects of Value and Contrast

From the time I first began quilting, traditional interlocking designs such as *Milky Way* and *Virginia Reel* intrigued me. I couldn't figure out how seemingly complex shapes could be made to interlock so perfectly. I wondered how I could create similar designs. When I began to study tessellations, I realized that the concept is very simple and can be broken into two steps: shading the pattern with light and dark contrasts and then applying the symmetries. As we shall see, value adds a completely new dimension, allowing tessellations to emerge, as if by magic, from patterns where none seemed to exist before.

Creating Tessellating Designs from Traditional Quilt Patterns

When looking at a line drawing of an individual unit of the *Virginia Reel* block, it is difficult to see how this seemingly intricate design can result from such a simple pattern. Most people tend to color that line drawing in a very traditional manner, creating a design such as the one in Illustration 9.12. However, to create the interlocking *Virginia Reel* pattern, the block is colored quite differently.

Shading Quarter Sections Light and Dark

Two exact and opposite quarter sections are shaded dark and the remaining two quarter sections are shaded light. The design now interlocks because those quarter sections now blend together to flow beyond strict quarter squares in each block. The completion of the pattern for *Virginia Reel* comes when four of the blocks

Virginia Reel, *Barbara Dean, 1995.*

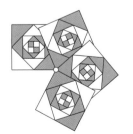

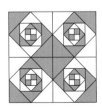

Tile that repeats for
pattern

Illustration 9.13. *Here the design has been shaded with opposite quarter sections light and dark. Then four of those squares have been rotated to produce the repeating tile.*

One-Motif Patterns

Translation (p1), midpoint rotation (p2)

Mirror (pm), glided staggered mirror (pmg). By recoloring, this same symmetry produces interlocking frogs instead of ram's horns.

Staggered mirror (cm), double mirror (pmm), glide (pg), double glide (pgg)

Two-Motif Patterns

Staggered double mirror (cmm) produces two interlocking tessellating motifs (left). Recoloring some of the motifs produces a more uniform arrangement of this pattern (right).

Another two-motif pattern can be created by rotating the original square four times (p4) and then mirroring the result.

Three-Motif Patterns

A three-motif pattern (pinwheels, frogs, and crabs) results from applying the mirrored pinwheel (p4g) symmetry.

Illustration 9.14. One-, two-, and three-motif patterns from Virginia Reel.

are rotated around one of the corners, thus creating the repeating tile, as shown in Illustration 9.13. Once I discovered the secret to shading the *Virginia Reel* block, I realized the same technique could be applied to any traditional quilt design. A whole new world of tessellating patterns emerged.

Furthermore, the exciting part about this technique of shading two opposite quarter sections of a block dark and the other two light is that you don't have to stop with a single design. With an understanding of the symmetrical arrangements of blocks it is easy to experiment further. By applying other symmetries to the same block, more tessellating patterns emerge. Because the unit itself has symmetry within the cell, several of the 11 symmetries that can be applied to a square will produce the same results. But there are still several different pattern possibilities that can be created, some forming one-

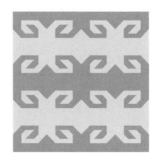

Virginia Reel
line drawing

Half-sections
shaded light
and dark

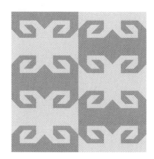

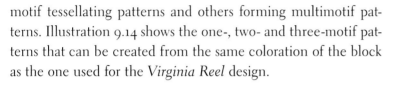

Double mirror (pmm)

Staggered double mirror (cmm)

motif tessellating patterns and others forming multimotif patterns. Illustration 9.14 shows the one-, two- and three-motif patterns that can be created from the same coloration of the block as the one used for the *Virginia Reel* design.

Shading Half-Sections Light and Dark

The examples in Illustration 9.14 are all based on dividing the traditional-style block into four equal sections and then shading alternate sections light and dark. For even more design possibilities, the same principle can be applied but instead of dividing the block into four sections, it can be divided into two sections, which are then colored light and dark. Working with the same *Virginia Reel* line drawing, Illustration 9.15 shows a few of the pattern possibilities with this technique. It is interesting to see how the identical block design can produce so many interlocking patterns.

Selecting Patterns to Transform

Any symmetrical design that is based on a square can be recolored in this manner to produce tessellating motifs. The main consideration is that the design must be capable of being broken up into quarters or halves. For example, the pattern for *Tesselocean* on the next page is actually derived from the traditional quilt block *Churn Dash*. However, to create four exact quarter sections, the central square has been divided into four smaller squares (Illustration 9.16). Two opposite quarter sections of the block are then colored light and the other two dark; that unit is rotated four times to get the repeating tile. Once again, additional symmetries can be applied to the block to achieve other patterns.

Pinwheel (p4)

Midpoint rotation (pg)

Illustration 9.15. Instead of coloring opposite quarter sections the same, try coloring opposite halves light and dark.

Tessel-ocean, *Terri Willett, 1996*

Traditional coloring for the Churn Dash *pattern will not form an interlocking design.*

To create the tessellating pattern in Tessel-ocean, *the center square is divided into four. The unit is colored and rotated to create the repeating tile.*

Illustration 9.16. *Various colorings of* Churn Dash.

There are a couple of additional factors to keep in mind when experimenting with these types of tessellations. First, within each colored section, make sure that there is an overall continuity between the dark or light portions. In other words, a dark portion of the design must always overlap another dark section. If you only have corners of shapes meet, the design becomes too busy. Second, work with fairly simple designs; they are more effective than complicated ones.

Illustration 9.17 shows some of the many possibilities using the traditional *Churn Dash* block. The key is to experiment. You'll find that once you begin by coloring even very traditional designs, you can achieve some wonderful effects.

Traditional coloring and layout of Churn Dash *pattern*

Milky Way variation

Pinwheel (p4)

Double mirror (pmm), mirrored pinwheel (p4g)

Opposite sections colored light and dark

Pinwheel (p4)

Double mirror (pmm), mirrored pinwheel (p4g)

Staggered mirror (cm)

Half-sections colored light and dark

Pinwheel (p4)

Midpoint rotation (pg)

Staggered mirror (cm)

Half-sections colored light and dark

Pinwheel (p4)

Double mirror (pmm)

Midpoint rotation (pg)

Illustration 9.17. A few of the many tessellating patterns that are possible by coloring the traditional quilt design Churn Dash *in different ways.*

Transforming *Evening Star*

Here, a traditional quilt block, *Evening Star*, has been shaded as described in the text, with opposite quarter sections alternating dark and light. The traditional version of this design is shown along with three of the many possible interlocking patterns that can be created using this technique. Study these designs and those on the previous page before experimenting with other quilt blocks. Shade each one in different ways for different effects.

Make sure within each colored section that there is continuity between the dark or light portions of the design. In other words, a dark section must always overlap another dark section. If only the corners meet, the design becomes too busy. As you experiment, choose simple designs, as they give more effective results than more complicated blocks.

Traditional-Style Tessellating Designs

This page contains some of my traditional-style tessellating designs. These can be made in the same way as regular quilt blocks. When they fit together side by side, they form interlocking patterns. The shaded version shows the light and dark placement that will allow the interlocking pattern to emerge.

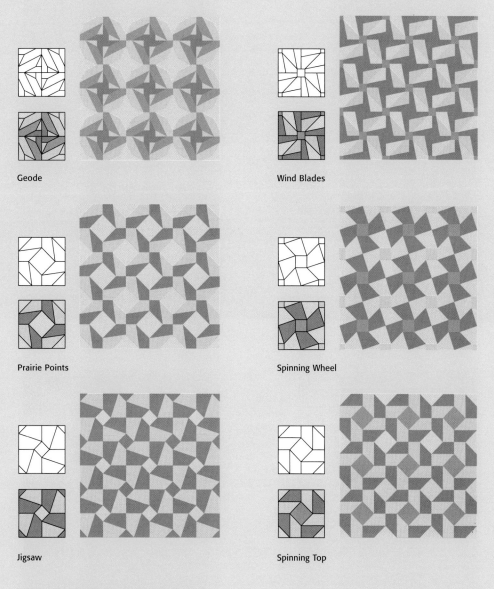

Geode

Wind Blades

Prairie Points

Spinning Wheel

Jigsaw

Spinning Top

---

1. For more information on drafting geometric designs see *Patchwork Patterns* EPM Publications © 1979 and *Patchwork Portfolio* EPM Publications © 1989 by this author.

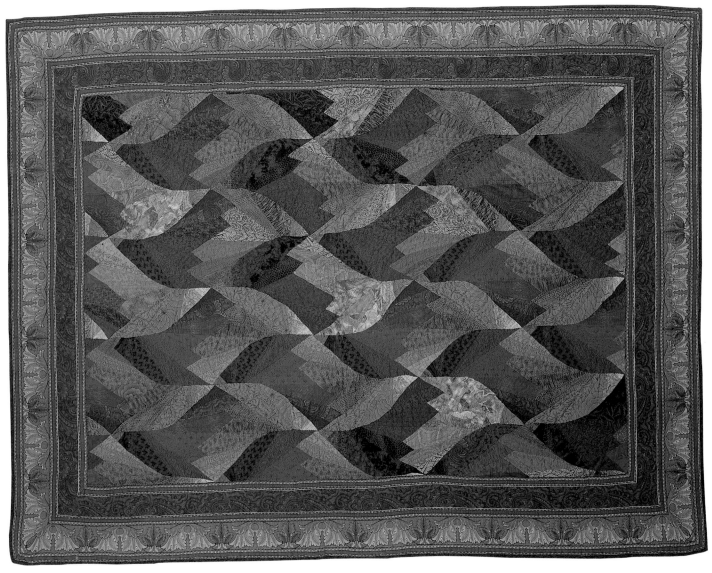

Soaring High, *Jinny Beyer*, 1998.

CHAPTER 10

Creating *Representational* Tessellations

W<small>HEN YOU FIRST SAW</small> E<small>SCHER'S</small> multimotif designs, where butterflies interlock perfectly or fish alternate with birds, you were probably just as perplexed as I was, but now that you have experimented with tessellating designs, you should not be so overwhelmed.

The very same principles we used to create geometric tessellations in the preceding chapter apply here. The key is to open your eyes and imagination. Look beyond the obvious to see the hint of an image, then let that image evolve into a design others will recognize.

How many times have you looked at a cloud and seen a castle, a monster, or an angel? Look at the tessellated images you create in the same way: if you have an inkling of what that shape might be, then you can develop the shape into reality.

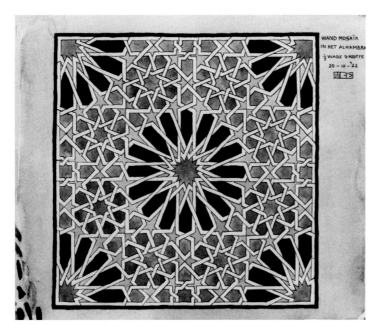

Illustration 10.1. Sketch of a wall mosaic in the Alhambra by M. C. Escher.

Escher's Vision

Maurits Cornelius Escher was the master of creating tessellations, and his work has intrigued people all over the world. Born in The Netherlands on June 17, 1898, he was fascinated with tessellating designs from a very early age. Upon completion of high school, he enrolled in the School for Architecture and Decorative Arts in Haarlem where he pursued a course in graphic arts.

But it was his visit to the Alhambra in Granada, Spain, when he was just 24 and a return visit 13 years later that altered the course of Escher's artistic career. In Spain, he studied the wonderful interlocking tilings that adorned the walls and floors of buildings. He was intrigued by how designs like this were created, yet he was surprised that they were limited to geometric forms. As he noted in his diary during his first trip: "The strange thing about this Moorish decoration is the total absence of any human or animal form—even almost of any plant form."[1]

Escher filled his notebook with sketches of the various geometric designs he found at the Alhambra and then embarked on a life journey of working to create recognizable forms—birds, animals, even people—that would fill a plane without any gaps or overlaps. From his notes and designs it is apparent that many of his images grew from the strictly geometric forms that he had sketched at the Alhambra and other places he visited.

1. Doris Schattschneider, *M. C. Escher: Visions of Symmetry* (New York: W. H. Freeman and Company, 1990), 9. This wonderful book gives an insight into Escher's life and artistic accomplishments. It reproduces Escher's previously unpublished notebooks along with working sketches of many of his tessellating designs. The book contains more than 400 illustrations of Escher's work and is extremely valuable to those who are searching for a greater understanding of how to create recognizable tessellations.

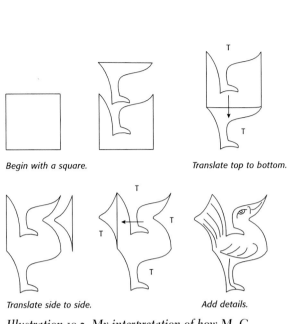

Begin with a square.   Translate top to bottom.

Translate side to side.   Add details.

Illustration 10.2. My interpretation of how M. C. Escher's bird design was created. Simply draw lines from the places where four birds meet, and the underlying grid of squares becomes apparent. By isolating a single square from the grid, you can see that this design was achieved through straight translation, top to bottom and side to side.

Symmetry Drawing E128 (*Birds*) *by M. C. Escher. Sketch from Escher's notebooks.*

Escher spent countless hours and days stretching his mind to make the representational images that have become his trademark—birds intertwined with fish, flowers interspersed with leaves, angels alternating with devils, multi-colored butterflies interlocking perfectly across a plane. He spent even more hours refining them. But in the end it was his innate talent that made his images come to life and attract aficionados from around the world. As Doris Schattschneider says, "Today computers can be programmed to apply geometric motions instantaneously to any squiggle or shape that is drawn on the screen—instant regular divisions of the plane. But the art of finding just the right squiggle, of seeing the possibilities for an imaginative creature in a rudimentary form is not programmable; it is a gift of special observation, ingenious imagination, and playful wit."[2]

---

2. Ibid., p. 108.

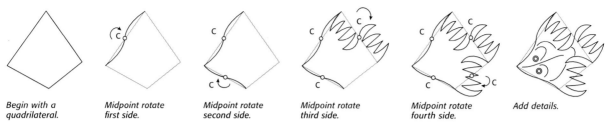

Begin with a quadrilateral.

Midpoint rotate first side.

Midpoint rotate second side.

Midpoint rotate third side.

Midpoint rotate fourth side.

Add details.

Illustration 10.3. My interpretation of Escher's fish design. Draw lines from the places where four fish meet and you will see an underlying grid of quadrilaterals. The design was achieved through midpoint rotation on four sides.

Escher's Techniques

There is no formula for creating tessellations that look like birds, animals, or other objects. It takes time and experimentation to come up with ideas that can be transformed into tessellating motifs. But a look at how Escher approached his work gives valuable insight into designing your own representational patterns.

Escher, who made most of his designs in the forms of living creatures, thought in terms of how the various animals are normally viewed—in profile, straight on, or from the top. This had an impact on how he would create them. For instance, people or horses are usually seen from the front or side and right side up. Escher seldom created them from any other viewpoint. He used simple operations like a translation from the bottom to the top or a glide from the bottom to the opposite side of quadrilaterals. On the other hand, birds, fish, insects, and reptiles can be viewed in a variety of ways, so to create images of these he used rotation freely.

Once Escher found a system for a specific shape—legs, wings, or fins, for example—he usually used the same cuts in multiple designs, making only slight changes and often mixing and matching them in his motifs. He found rotation a very powerful tool. Of the 83 one-motif designs shown in Doris Schattschneider's book, 55 of them use some form of rotation. Thirty-eight of those 55 use midpoint rotation, which seems to have been Escher's favorite manipulation in his one-motif patterns. It should be noted that two thirds of the time the midpoint rotation was done on a shape that contained no right angles. Illustration 10.3 shows the sequence Escher used to cre-

Symmetry Drawing E90, *(Fish Design) by M. C. Escher.*

ate the fish motif opposite. At first glance, one might think the image results from glide symmetry. Yet closer examination shows that Escher midpoint rotated each side of a quadrilateral. He used similar cuts for other motifs depicting fins of fish or wings of birds. Study of these may help you when trying to create your own recognizable tessellations.

Of the shapes Escher used to create his representational motifs, it seems that the quadrilateral was most popular. It is important to note that he seemed to prefer a skewed parallelogram to a true rectangle or square. Other favorite shapes were the kite, the equilateral triangle, and the right triangle. While many of his designs contain other shapes, these were the ones he most commonly used.

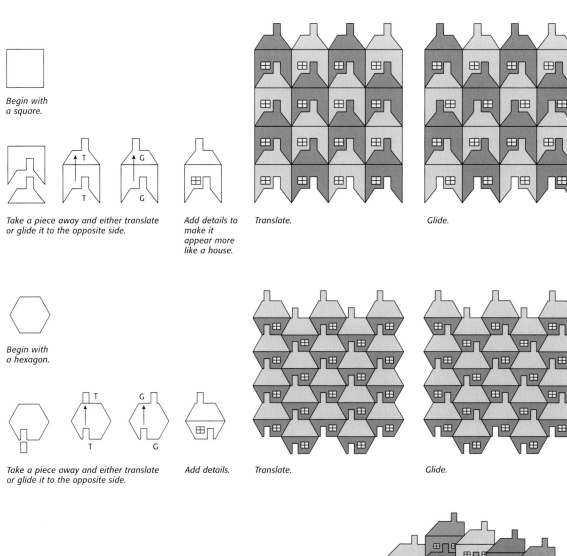

Begin with a square.

Take a piece away and either translate or glide it to the opposite side.

Add details to make it appear more like a house.

Translate.

Glide.

Begin with a hexagon.

Take a piece away and either translate or glide it to the opposite side.

Add details.

Translate.

Glide.

Begin with a square that is turned 15°.

Take a piece away from the bottom, and translate it to the opposite side.

Take a piece away from the right side, and translate it to the left side.

Add details.

Translate.

Illustration 10.4. Houses drawn from a square, a hexagon, and a skewed square.

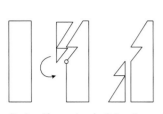 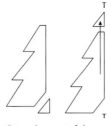 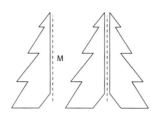 

Begin with a rectangle. Cut a piece out of half of one side, and midpoint rotate to the other half of the side.

Cut a piece out of the bottom, and translate it to the top.

Mirror the unaltered side.

Draw lines to all the inward angles for ease of sewing.

Making Representational Tessellations

There are various ways to create representational tessellations, as we shall see, but the principles are exactly the same as those that guide the design from simple shapes of geometric patterns that interlock. Experimentation is part of the challenge, and the results are always worth the effort.

One of the easiest ways to create a representational tessellation is to begin with the simplest symmetry operations, such as a translation from one side to another or with a glide from one side to the opposite side.

To create tessellating houses or buildings, begin by drawing the outline of the rooftops and then translate or glide that to the opposite side. The addition of doors or windows will add elements that will help make the image realistic. Three house variations are shown in Illustration 10.4, the first created from a square, the second from a hexagon, and the third also from a square. The first two show the differences in how a pattern looks, depending on whether the side that is changed is translated or glided. The third design shows how different the pattern can look if the square is rotated before the change takes place.

Mirroring a motif often produces representational images such as bats, birds, or butterflies. With mirroring, you can create half of an image and leave one side free of alteration to be mirrored later as in *Enchanted Forest* in Illustration 10.5.

Illustration 10.5. Detail from Enchanted Forest *(page 124). A combination of techniques—midpoint rotation, translation, and mirror—were used to create this pattern.*

Simple Representational Motifs

Tessellating Sue, *Jinny Beyer. A computer-generated quilt design.*

Begin with a rectangle.

Take a piece from one side of the rectangle and translate it to the opposite side.

Next, take a piece from the half of one of the two remaining sides, and midpoint rotate it to the other half side.

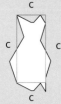

Take a piece from half of the remaining side, and midpoint rotate it to the other half of the side.

Make any changes to the interior of the shape.

The first representational tessellation I created was *Sun Bonnet Sue*. During the 1920s and 1930s and even into the 1940s, this popular quilt pattern depicted a girl with wide dress and large bonnet. I experimented with a variety of shapes until I decided that a rectangle would give me the best chance of creating a recognizable Sue, as shown. Once the outline was complete, I realized it had some similarity to a cat sitting on its haunches and others thought they saw a fish. The final three drawings show the images.

Look at the quilt right side up or on its side to see the three motifs. Something similar happens in *Girl with Bonnet*. If the design is turned upside down, the pattern resembles baskets.

Girl with Bonnet, *Carole Nicholas, 1998.*

To create
women with
hats, begin with
a right triangle.

Alter one
side of the
triangle.

Glide that
to the other
equal side.

Mirror the long side
of the triangle.

Finished shape

Alter the inside to
look like women
with hats.

Or turn upside
down and make
a basket.

Animal faces can be created fairly easily. Begin with a square
and draw the ears of a fox, cat, dog, or rabbit and translate them.
When multiple designs are put together, the animal faces appear to
overlap. Experiment with how the design looks when it is translated
or glided or with the original shape slightly skewed.

 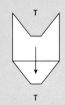 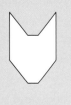 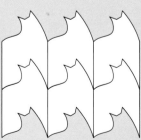 

For a fox, or dog, begin with a
square and take a piece away that
represents the ears of the animal.

Translate that
piece to produce
the chin.

Completed
shape.

For a cat, translate ears and a
head from the bottom to the top.

Black Spruce, *Jinny Beyer. A design based on translation of a hexagon.*

Translate all sides of the hexagon.

For graphic design, alter inside to enhance the tree.

For fabric, glass, or other mediums that require separate pieces, draw lines from inward angles.

Illustration 10.6. Creating Black Spruce.

When designing *Enchanted Forest* (page 207), I worked to get a tessellation that looked like an evergreen tree. Beginning with a rectangle, I performed a midpoint rotation on one of the long sides and translated a piece from the bottom to the top. Finally, I mirrored the non-altered long edge of the rectangle. Color choices help emphasize the design; subtle shades of green fabrics help make the trees stand out, while blue and teal fabrics put the sky into relief.

Once you become comfortable with each symmetry operation and know what to expect, use it again and again with the objective of creating representational shapes. When you find a method for making wings or fins, for example, keep experimenting with it. Then, find out how a cut that gave you a representational tessellation when working on a square works on a parallelogram, a kite shape, or on a diamond.

Let the Motif Dictate the Design

An alternative to working toward a specific representational image is simply to experiment with various shapes, altering the sides in different ways and just waiting to see what happens. Very often a shape created in this way will end up looking vaguely like something else. By refining some of the cuts, you can make the image more apparent, and adding lines to the inside of the shape makes it even more recognizable. When you arrive at a shape, turn it in every direction to see if it reminds you of anything. If it does, go from there. Refining an image is much easier than creating one from scratch.

While experimenting with tessellations based on a hexagon, I translated all sides, and suddenly there was a design that looked to me like a pine tree. I experimented with color and soon saw

Begin with a 60° diamond.   *Cut a piece out of one side, and rotate it around the 120° angle.*   *Cut a piece out of another side.*

Rotate that piece around the other 120° angle.   *Completed tile*   *Dotted line indicates one more seam is needed for sewing.*

Illustration 10.7. Creating Sport.

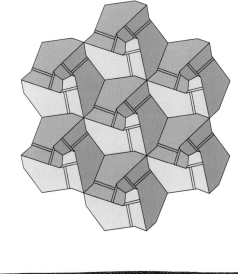

Sport, *Jinny Beyer, 1997.*

an irregularly shaped evergreen that was reminiscent of the distinctive black spruce trees of Alaska. The tree in *Black Spruce,* Illustration 10.6, is more interesting than the tree I designed for *Enchanted Forest* because the design is not so regular. Trees do not have completely equal balance on every branch. It is the break in symmetry—the unequal branches—that makes the tree that I came upon by happenstance for *Black Spruce* more exciting than the one I worked so hard to design in *Enchanted Forest.*

The beginning shape for creating the horse in *Sport* was a 60° diamond. Rotations were done around each of the 120° angles to create the motif. I then looked at the shape in terms of how it had to be broken up for sewing and drew lines from the inward angles that not only broke the shape up for piecing but also represented the halter. The completed quilt was intriguing in that each horse looked as if the horse next to it was actually the body of the first and that the first horse was wearing a blanket (Illustration 10.7).

Opposites Attract, *Danielle Brower-Naber, 1996.*

G1   G1   G2   G1   G2

Begin with a 60° diamond.   *Cut a piece out and flip it.*   *Give it back to another side.*   *Cut a piece out of one of the remaining sides and flip it.*   *Give it back to the last side.*   *Completed shape.*

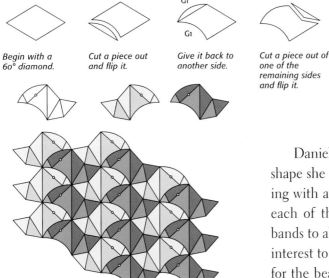

Illustration 10.8. Creating Opposites Attract.

Danielle Brouwer-Naber saw birds in the tessellating shape she created for her quilt *Opposites Attract.* Working with a 60° diamond she did two glides, one around each of the 60° angles. She broke the shape up into bands to allow for ease of piecing as well as to give extra interest to the shading of the colors in each bird. A line for the beak and a button for the eye give the finishing touches to make the birds recognizable to anyone who views the quilt.

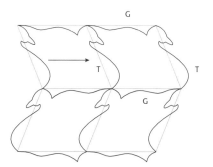

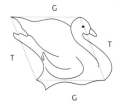

The piece being translated can go outside and inside the original shape.

Work from a Grid of Geometric Shapes

Once you understand how to create tessellating motifs by working with cuts from individual shapes, you may want to begin working from an underlying grid, as this allows more freedom of design. If you work from an underlying grid, any alteration can occur, whether or not it lies inside the original shape. Whatever you draw can be moved to one of the other sides, as long as that side is equal in length to the side from which it

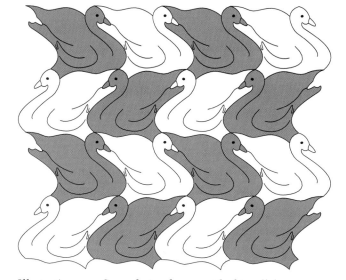

Illustration 10.9. Swan design from a grid of parallelograms.

is receiving the shape. When creating recognizable motifs, this is a very important consideration. Working from a grid, while a little more cumbersome in terms of re-creating the motif over and over, can offer more design options.

The swan design shown here was created from a grid of parallelograms. Working with two sheets of tracing paper placed over the grid, I drew the beak and breast of the bird along one of the lines. The line fell both inside and outside of the parallelogram. I traced this same line onto a second piece of tracing paper, then moved that piece over so that I could trace the line again on the opposite side of the parallelogram. Next I experimented with the top of the shape trying to achieve a line that would resemble the back and tail of the swan. When I was satisfied, once again working with the two pieces of tracing paper, I glided that top line to the bottom.

Piece cut from square and rotated that produced original design.

Piece with curved angles that produces the butterfly design.

Four cells rotated to form the tile.

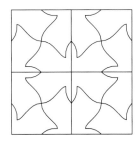

Four groups of rotated cells are double mirrored to create the pattern.

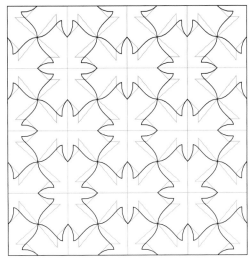

Mirrored pinwheel (p4g) symmetry applied to four of the groups of rotated cells creates the design.

Illustration 10.10. Creating a butterfly design from a square.

Changes were made to the inside of the motif to make it look more like a butterfly.

Use Your Imagination

One of the easiest ways to create recognizable tessellating designs is just to let them happen. Use your imagination to create from the outline of a shape or grid a whimsical or decorative object. A grid of repeating tessellating shapes may suggest an outline of a motif, which will in turn lead to small alterations that help emphasize the original idea. An open mind is essential.

The patterns on page 5 show various design possibilities that occur when just one piece is cut from a square. I went back to those designs to see if any of the overall patterns reminded me of any recognizable shapes. I could see a hint of butterflies in number 15, which we can now identify as a mirrored pinwheel (p4g) symmetry pattern, but realized that I would need some curved lines instead of the angular ones to illustrate a more realistic wing. The head was was too fat, so I placed a piece of tracing paper over the pattern and, drawing over what had been the original cut in the square, made the head narrower and slightly curved. Then I made a soft curve in the area that looked like wings. By placing the tracing paper over the existing pattern, it

Rotating the piece to the left instead of right and applying mirrored pinwheel symmetry motions produces crabs, not butterflies.

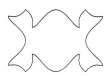

Rotate four of the altered cells.

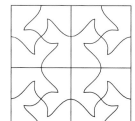

Double mirroring that group of cells creates the pattern.

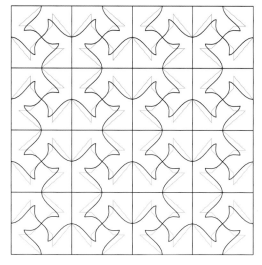
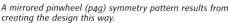

A mirrored pinwheel (p4g) symmetry pattern results from creating the design this way.

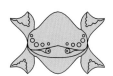

Detailing the inside of the shape makes it look like a crab.

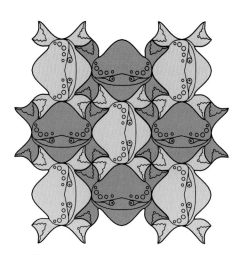

Illustration 10.11. Creating a crab design from the same square.

was easy to see how the changes affected the adjacent motif. Working with a second piece of tracing paper, I copied this new section, rotated the top piece of tracing paper until I had four of the pieces drawn, then flipped the tracing paper and kept tracing the motif to re-create the original symmetry. After a few tries, I was satisfied with the outline of the butterfly. I added details inside the shape to make the butterfly more apparent.

Next I wondered what would happen if I took this refined alteration to the original square and applied additional symmetry motions to see if other recognizable motifs occurred as well. For the butterfly design in Illustration 10.10, I used mirrored pinwheel (p4g) symmetry motions on a simple square. The design was created by cutting a piece away from the bottom of the square and rotating it around the bottom *right* corner. If the same symmetry motions are applied, but the piece is rotated around the bottom *left* corner, the design resembles crabs instead (Illustration 10.11).

It is interesting to note that pattern 17 on page 5, which was created by rotating the piece around the bottom right corner, rotating four of those, then mirroring the result, also produced

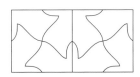

Piece cut from a square. Change hard edges to a curve.   *Rotate four of the altered cells.*   *Then mirror that for the tile.*

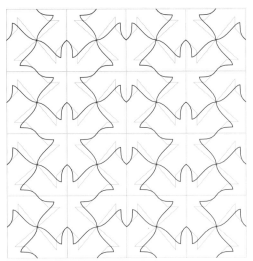

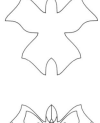

Detailing makes the shape recognizable as a butterfly.

Working with the cell in this manner creates a glided staggered mirror symmetry (pmg) pattern.

Illustration 10.12. Using a grid for an alternate butterfly design.

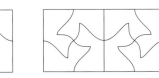

Rotating to left instead of right and then mirroring four of those rotated cells produces frogs, not butterflies.   *Rotate four of the altered cells.*   *Tile*

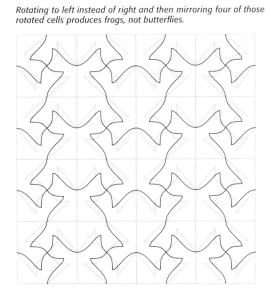

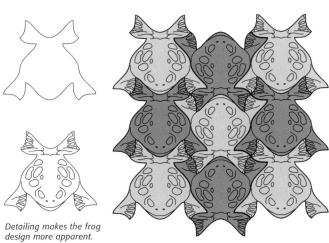

Detailing makes the frog design more apparent.

A glided staggered mirror (pmg) symmetry pattern results from creating the design in this way.

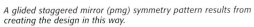

Illustration 10.13. Using a different rotation to create the frog design.

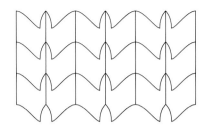

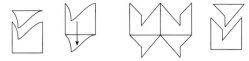

Begin with pattern 7 from page 5, and turn it upside down. Change hard lines to curves. .

Once pattern 7 has been altered with the curve, there is a faint impression of a bird.

Further alterations can emphasize the head and beak.

what looked like a butterfly, although it was a different shape. (Illustration 10.12). When the piece was rotated around the *left* corner instead (as in Illustration 10.13) the design looks like frogs.

Beginning again with the same piece cut from a square, I next did a translation and mirrored it. The shape of a bird began to emerge, but the straight sides needed some curve, and the bird needed a beak. I did a midpoint rotation on the side and changed the head to allow for a beak (Illustration 10.14). I soon began to realize how Escher must have felt when he found one curve or angle that worked for him and how that must have led to others until eventually a completely different design emerged. Here is how he described that discovery:

A midpoint rotation on the side can delineate wings.

> One can divide a plane into geometric shapes according to certain systems; these forms can become infinitely varied and very complex and still meet the requirement of filling the plane without congruent form in rhythmic repetition without leaving any void. If one then tries to mold the form so as to evoke an association with something familiar to the viewer—an object, an animal, or whatever it might be—it becomes a compelling game in view of the infinite possibilities offered as well as the rigorous restrictions imposed by the rules. It is a painstaking process of groping and fumbling about. Sometimes not a single one of the patterns that appear at the end were consciously sought at the start. It dawns on you slowly. Then comes the moment you recognize it, when you suddenly realize. . . it is a man on a horse! After this he develops rapidly under the impact of certainty.[3]

A mirror will complete the outline of the bird.

Fill in details to further emphasize the image of the bird.

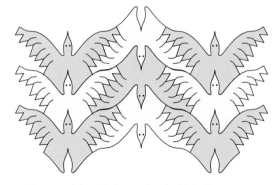

Because of the midpoint rotation, the birds alternate flying one direction or another.

Illustration 10.14. Creating a bird design.

Escher admitted that very often a design just evolved when he was seeking no particular motif. That is one of the most exciting aspects of creating tessellations of your own.

3. Schattschneider, *M. C. Escher: Visions of Symmetry*, p. 110.

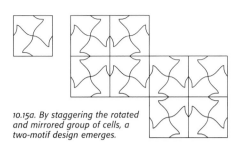

10.15a. By staggering the rotated and mirrored group of cells, a two-motif design emerges.

Two interlocking butterfly motifs

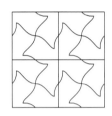

10.15b. A three-motif design can be created by rotating or translating four of the original motifs, which will result in the same design.

Rotate four of them or translate four of them for the same result.

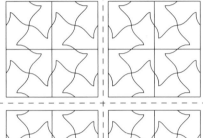

Then double mirror the four units on all sides.

Three butterflies intertwined

Illustration 10.15. Using a grid to create two- and three-motif designs.

Multimotif Designs

While we are all fascinated with the interlocking birds, fish, reptiles, and other creatures that Escher created, even more intriguing are his two-, three-, or four-motif designs. Of the 137 Escher designs I studied in Doris Schattschneider's *M. C. Escher: Visions of Symmetry*, 54 of them contain two or more tessellating motifs.

With an understanding of translation, rotation, glide, and mirror, we can begin to see how Escher created many of his designs, but the designs he evolved with two or more motifs are amazing. What did he do? Where did the change occur? What shape did he begin with? It is not as complex as it seems. Indeed, Escher may have found that two-motif designs in recognizable shapes were easier to design than were one-motif patterns

Using Grids for Multimotif Designs

The easiest way to create multimotif designs is to use a grid. Earlier we saw how working with an underlying grid allows recognizable shapes to emerge from a design. Look again at Illustration 10.10 to see how pattern 15 gave the suggestion of a butterfly, and the original design was modified to look more like one. Then, look at Illustration 10.12 to see how, when other symmetry motions are applied to pattern 17, a different butterfly emerges. If staggered double mirror (cmm) symmetry motions are applied to the rotated tile, then the two butterflies in designs 15 and 17 come together in one pattern (Illustration 10.15a).

It is possible to go a step further and create a design with three tessellating motifs, this time with three different butterflies intertwined. The design is created by taking the original rotated square and rotating or translating four of those. They are then double mirrored as shown (Illustration 10.15b).

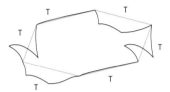

Translate all sides.

Create two motifs inside shape.

Illustration 10.16. Symmetry Drawing E72 by M. C. Escher, and my interpretation of how he achieved this design, from a hexagonal shape.

Escher's Multimotif Designs

The main way in which Escher created his multimotif designs involved creating outlines of motifs by translations, rotations, and glides in much the same way as he did with his one-motif designs. But this time instead of detailing the inside of that outline to accentuate one representational image, he broke it up with two or more images. This created more versatility in terms of what could be done inside the tessellating outline, since that could be arbitrary and would not affect how the shapes fit together. With Escher's one-motif designs, he created tessellating shapes that usually looked very similar to the creature and then refined the images with lines inside the shape. This is

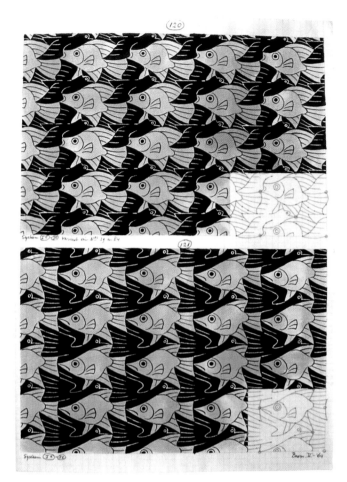

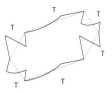

Illustration 10.17. **Symmetry Drawing E120** *and* **Symmetry Drawing E121** *by M.C. Escher, and my interpretation of how he achieved this design from a hexagonal shape.*

immediately evident, for example, when looking at Escher's bird on page 203 or his fish on page 205. With most of his two-motif designs, however, it is fairly difficult to determine what the representational motifs are just by looking at the outline. Two such examples are shown here. One shows fish jumping into sailboats (Illustration 10.16). The other shows a combination of fish and birds (Illustration 10.17). The illustrations show how the outlines of the shapes can be created, but it is very difficult to determine the motifs from the outline alone. It is only once that outline is split into two shapes that the motif becomes apparent. Another major factor in recognition comes in the detailing that Escher added *inside* the shape. In the first example, detailing the bows and sails on the boat and on the second, detailing the eye and fins of the fish bring the motif to life. The imagination can take off and do anything to the inside of the shape and that will not change how the outline itself tessellates and fills the surface.

It is interesting to note that although Escher used rotation freely in his one-motif designs that are shown in the Schattschneider book (55 out of 83 contain rotation), only 12 out of 54 of his multimotif designs contain rotation. Translation was clearly his favorite means of manipulating shapes in his two-or-

Symmetry Drawing E119, *by M. C. Escher.*

more-motif designs, as 24 out of the 54 were created entirely with translation and five were a combination of translations and glides.

Why did Escher treat his one-motif and multimotif designs differently? Perhaps it has to do with the fact that single-motif designs containing all translations can appear a little static. Everything is lined up in rows, and there is little freedom of movement. Rotations and glides can add flow and interest, and this could be why Escher seemed to prefer those in his one-motif designs.

But the two-or-more-motif designs needed some order to help distinguish the figures, which is perhaps why Escher used quite a few translations. He then created flow and interest by the way in which he broke up the inside of the shape. Many of his two-motif designs have one motif facing one direction and the other one facing the opposite direction, as in the example of birds and fish (Illustration 10.17). These types of designs can fool us into thinking that there must be a glide involved, but study of the outline reveals strict translation.

The reason for focusing on the way Escher worked is that he spent years developing his designs, determining which methods worked best for him. Perhaps beginning the same way in your own experiments will help you achieve single-motif and multimotif designs a little more quickly as you learn from Escher's techniques. As you work, the detail, the balance, and the cleverness of Escher's designs will inspire and delight you.

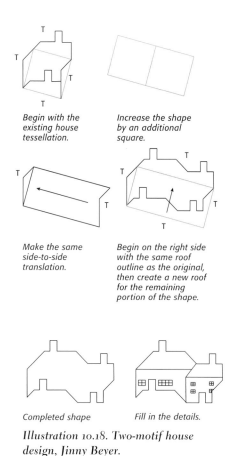

Begin with the
existing house
tessellation.

Increase the shape
by an additional
square.

Make the same
side-to-side
translation.

Begin on the right side
with the same roof
outline as the original,
then create a new roof
for the remaining
portion of the shape.

Completed shape

Fill in the details.

*Illustration 10.18. Two-motif house
design, Jinny Beyer.*

Experimenting with Multimotif Designs

To experiment with two-motif designs, try translating one part of a recognizable motif on one side (head, fins, wings, petals, etc.) and a part of another recognizable motif on the remaining two sides. Then just keep working with the inside until you blend the two objects together into recognizable forms. If you have trouble making the motifs fit or work together, try varying the original shape. Instead of a rectangle, see what happens when it is skewed into a parallelogram. Or make the shape thicker or narrower, and then try the translations again.

I approached the tessellation in Illustration 10.18 a little differently. In creating a simple two-house design, I worked the single house-motif tessellations on page 206. The shapes from the original tessellation were increased to allow space for the extra motif. Then I made the same side-to-side translation on the new shape as I had on the original. I began with the same bottom-to-top translation as well, but had to add an additional roof line. Details were added within the final shapes to complete the design.

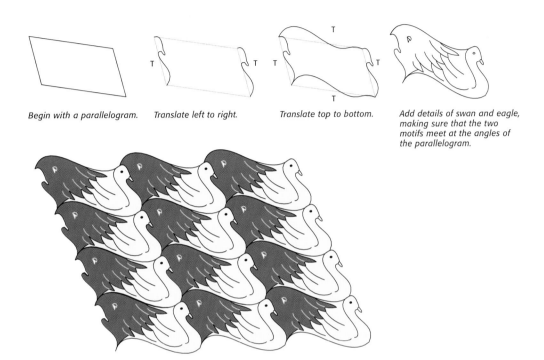

Begin with a parallelogram. *Translate left to right.* *Translate top to bottom.* *Add details of swan and eagle, making sure that the two motifs meet at the angles of the parallelogram.*

Illustration 10.19. A two-motif design, Endangered Species, *by Jinny Beyer.*

Moving from Single to Double Motifs

If you have created a single-motif design with a recognizable shape, you might want to take part of that motif for your two-motif design. That is what I did with *Endangered Species* in Illustration 10.19. I had previously designed the tessellating swan, shown on page 213, so I took the same line I had used for the head and breast of the swan and translated that from one side of a long parallelogram to the other. Since I planned to create two motifs, I worked with an elongated shape so there would be room for the two designs. The one side of the shape could be created into another swan, but I had to decide what the opposite side looked like so that I could alter the inside accordingly. Since nothing came to mind, I worked with translating the top and bottom of the shape and eventually came upon an image that looked like it could be the head of a frog, reptile, or large bird. I added details to complete the swan and eagle's head. Note that dark and light shading helps emphasize the two motifs.

Illustration 10.20. Symmetry Drawing E81 by M. C. Escher, and my interpretation of how he achieved this design. This is an example of double mirror (pmm) symmetry.

Making Motifs Stand Out

When creating two-motif designs, pay attention to where lines that separate the motifs hit the edge of the original shape. To be distinguishable, the individual motifs need separation from one another and this occurs with color and contrasts. This is very similar to the way color and contrasts are important in single-motif designs, as explained on page 170. If the motifs overlap each other at places other than where the shapes would normally join (at the angles of the shapes), when working with only light and dark contrasts, the image can become confused and individual motifs may not be discernible.

Two different multimotif designs are shown on pages 222 and 223. *Endangered Species* can be colored with all the eagles dark and the swans light, since the division of the two motifs go to angles on the original parallelogram. The houses, on the other hand, must have dark, medium, and light coloring for the motifs to stand out, because the division of the different motifs does not go to the angles of the original rectangle.

Mirroring to Create Multimotif Designs

A second way in which Escher created his multimotif designs is a method often used in designing geometric patterns: mirroring all sides of a shape. Some people may find this method easier; others will find it more difficult. In essence, the emerging design does not grow out of a transformation of the sides of a shape at all, but rather the entire design is created freeform, so to speak, within the shape.

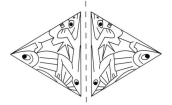

Illustration 10.21. Symmetry Drawing E85, by M. C. Escher and an interpretation of how this design was achieved.

Four of the 17 symmetries can be created by putting mirrors on all sides of the primary cell. These are the double mirror (pmm), which begins with a square; a mirror and three rotations (p3m1), which begins with an equilateral triangle; the traditional block (p4m), which begins with a right triangle; and the kaleidoscope (p6m), which begins with a 90°, 60°, 30° triangle. Interlocking images can be made from these shapes by creating half of a figure along one of the sides of the shape. The figure must begin at the corners of the shape, and one half figure will be made for each side of the shape.

Escher used this technique in Illustration 10.20, which depicts interlocking bees, butterflies, bats, and birds. A single square that contains half of each of the four motifs is shown along with the overall design. Note that the heads and tails of each motif begin and end at the angles of the square. The use of

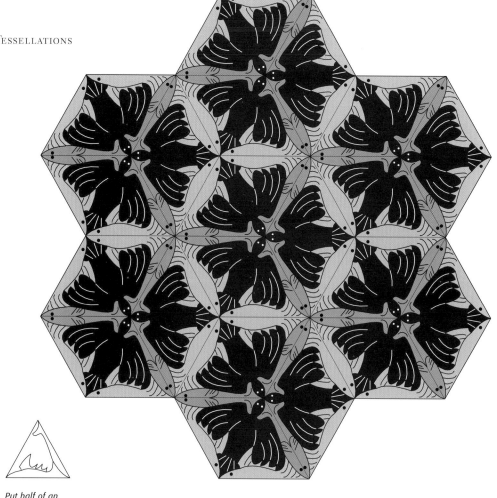

Begin with a triangle.

Put half of an image along each of the sides.

Fill in details.

Color light, medium, and dark, then mirror all sides.

Illustration 10.22. Birds and Fish, by Jinny Beyer. A three-motif interlocking pattern from an equilateral triangle.

the heavy black line helped so that a little more detail could be added to the shape.

Escher used a similar technique, but this time with an equilateral triangle, in Illustration 10.21. This pattern, an example of mirror and three rotations symmetry (p3m1) has halves of three motifs drawn on each side of the triangle.

The same technique can be used with the other shapes that allow a design to be created by mirroring all its sides. One of the easiest ways to begin is by drawing half of a very recognizable shape along one of the sides, making sure that the motif begins and ends at the corners of the shape. Then study the negative space that remains on the other sides to see if there is a suggestion of another motif. Remember that a lot can be done to the *inside* of the motif to make it more recognizable.

Two of my designs are shown in Illustrations 10.22 and 10.23. In the first one I used an equilateral triangle and began with the outline of half a bird. After studying the remaining negative space, I added a fish to each of the other sides. I had to make refinements to the bird until the three motifs joined together.

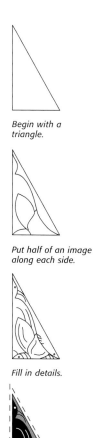

Begin with a triangle.

Put half of an image along each side.

Fill in details.

Color light, medium, and dark, then mirror all sides.

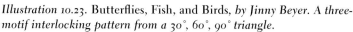

Illustration 10.23. Butterflies, Fish, and Birds, *by Jinny Beyer. A three-motif interlocking pattern from a 30°, 60°, 90° triangle.*

The second design begins with a 30°, 60°, 90° triangle and has birds, butterflies, and fish. I began by drawing a half of a butterfly, then changed it as I added the outline of a bird and a fish. The details make the motifs more recognizable.

At first glance, designs like these seem extraordinarily complex. Before I began to study tessellations and symmetry groups, I would not have even attempted or imagined patterns like these. You may have felt the same way when you picked up this book. Yet once you are able to analyze multimotif designs, to isolate their individual components, and to recognize the symmetry operations that complete them, you will realize that similar designs are within your reach.

Reptiles, *by M. C. Escher.*

CHAPTER 11

Metamorphosis

WE HAVE A SMALL POND in our backyard that is home to a wide variety of frogs and toads. It is fascinating to watch the tiny tadpoles as they gradually change into frogs and suddenly leap from the pond. Some of Escher's drawings remind me of this marvel of nature. For many, his most intriguing works are those where one tessellating motif mysteriously transforms into another. The design races across the surface, tricking the eye as it magically changes shape. This chapter shows how to make visual transformations like these both with geometric and representational motifs.

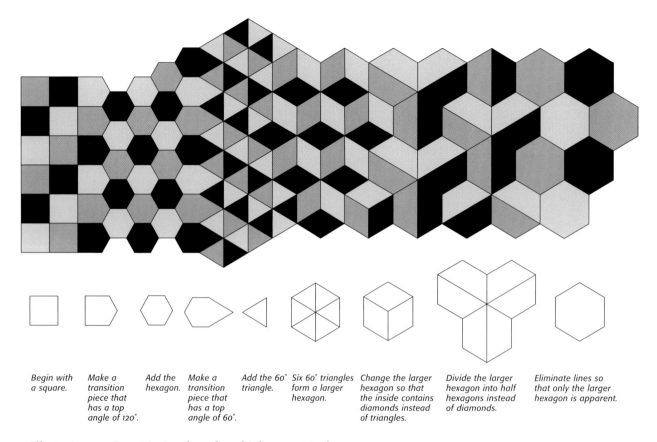

Begin with a square.

Make a transition piece that has a top angle of 120°.

Add the hexagon.

Make a transition piece that has a top angle of 60°.

Add the 60° triangle.

Six 60° triangles form a larger hexagon.

Change the larger hexagon so that the inside contains diamonds instead of triangles.

Divide the larger hexagon into half hexagons instead of diamonds.

Eliminate lines so that only the larger hexagon is apparent.

Illustration 11.1. *Transitioning through multiple geometric shapes.*

Moving from One Geometric Shape to Another

The easiest way to see how Escher achieved a visual metamorphosis in his representational images is to look first at the same types of transitions in geometric designs. Going from one geometric shape to another involves what I call *transition pieces*, as portions of each adjacent shape interlock to give flow to the design. Illustration 11.1 shows a transformation from left to right, as squares transform into hexagons, then transition into equilateral triangles, diamonds, half hexagons, and finally into larger hexagons. Work from the left side of the illustration to the right. Try experimenting with a wide number of shapes to achieve similar transformations.

Kaye-Oss, *Kaye Rhodes, 1992. The design of this quilt transitions smoothly from one shape into another.*

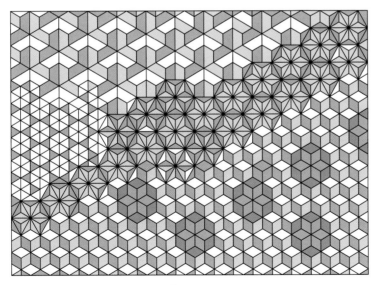

Illustration 11.2. Creating Kaye-Oss.

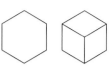

Four shapes make up the main part of Judy's quilt. These are all related to each other in size. The three-sided tessellating shape is created from an equilateral triangle and the other tessellating shape is created from a rectangle.

The three diamonds forming the baby blocks are based on a hexagon.

An equilateral triangle is drawn inside the hexagon and that triangle is the shape used for the blade design. All three sides of the triangle are midpoint rotated with the same cut.

Two sides of the rectangle are midpoint rotated for the other tessellating shape.

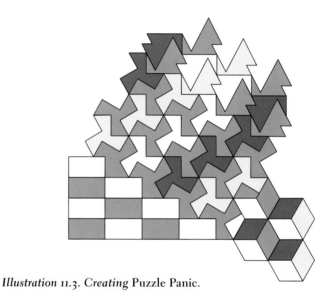

Illustration 11.3. Creating Puzzle Panic.

The quilt *Kaye-Oss* on page 231 uses this technique of moving from one shape to another very effectively. Working from an underlying grid of hexagons, the quilt transitions seamlessly from stars to building blocks to a variety of other designs. As Illustration 11.2 shows, these are all basic geometric shapes but these simple transitions add a sense of movement that makes the quilt dynamic.

Another way to make a transformation is to interlock common geometric shapes with tessellating motifs. The key is to work with shapes that are similar in size so that the sides can blend, as in *Puzzle Panic*. Illustration 11.3 demonstrates how the shapes were created and how the transitions were made. The

Puzzle Panic, *Judy Spahn, 1992. This quilt illustrates how to move from one shape to another.*

design moves from 60° diamonds, six of which form a hexagon, to blades. But the blade motif is related to the hexagon in that it is created from an equilateral triangle that fits within the original hexagon. A corner of a rectangle nestles into the right angle of the blade, and then that rectangle is transposed into another interlocking motif. The quilt has a wonderful effect of fluidity, as one shape flows into the next, tracking the eye across the design. Yet all shapes are based on simple geometrics. The transformation is miraculous.

Illustration 11.4. Creating a house with a simple tessellation.

Moving from Geometric Shapes to Representational Images

The basic principle of creating a design where one tessellating image changes to another is to make the changes to the shape gradually. Let's begin with a very simple example, where a square tessellates into an easily identifiable image of a house. In Illustration 11.4, we begin at the bottom with a row of squares. In row 2, to transition, there must be a straight edge that attaches to the top side of the square. Therefore, instead of taking a piece away, first add the desired piece to alter the shape. In effect, you have to jump ahead and give a piece back before it is taken away. Next, in row 3, take the identical piece away. The outline of a house begins to appear, as the piece that was given back in row two has been taken away. The exact same technique is repeated in rows 4, 5, and 6: a chimney is added in row 5 and taken away from the next shape in row 6. The design is gradually refined until the top row shows details on the inside of the shape. A tessellating row of houses emerges. The key is that, working from the bottom up, no matter what shape is added next, the bottom side of that shape must nestle into the top of the shape directly below.

A similar transformation takes place in Illustration 11.5. This time, a right triangle changes into a square and then gradually into interlocking cats. Since the cat motif is created by a double glide, the motifs must be reversed in alternate rows. The metamorphosis takes place in columns, with every one or two columns containing slight alterations to the shape. As shown, the transformation moves through eight shapes, ending with the final cat motif.

The piece is taken away, glided, and given back to the left side.

Another glide is performed to add a curve to the back.

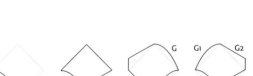
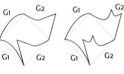

| Square | Add a curved piece to the square. | Take away the curved piece that was added to the previous square for column 5. | Take away a portion of the head in column 7. | Flip and add a portion of the head in column 8. | Take away and add back both the curved piece and the head portion. | Change a little more of the head. | Completed cat |

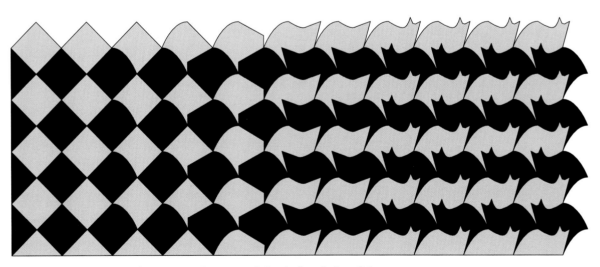

To transform squares into cats, the pieces are taken away and given back gradually until the cat is complete. Eight different shapes were used to complete the design.

Illustration 11.5. Cats, *by Jinny Beyer.*

Metamorphosis, *by M. C. Escher.*

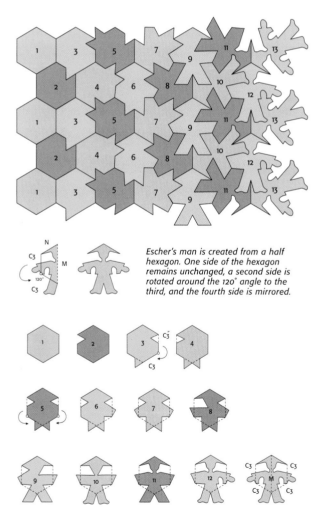

Escher's man is created from a half hexagon. One side of the hexagon remains unchanged, a second side is rotated around the 120° angle to the third, and the fourth side is mirrored.

Thirteen motifs make up the transition pieces. These pieces rotate around the hats of the men. The pieces are flipped every other row, odd numbers facing one way, even numbers, the other.

Illustration 11.6. Creating Metamorphosis.

Escher's Metamorphosis

No discussion of Escher's work would be complete without including one of his incredible designs, where representational images transform from one into the next as the design progresses. In *Metamorphosis*, Escher achieves this type of transformation in a masterful way. As you look at this sensational image, remember that the principle that makes it work is exactly the same as in the illustrations we have already examined in this chapter. Just as we progressed from one geometric shape into another, Escher moves effortlessly from one tessellating motif to the next, making changes—some gradual and some abrupt—to the motifs as they interlock across the surface.

In *Metamorphosis*, Escher extracts from his highly detailed drawing of a village basic geometric shapes which then flow into building blocks, then into hexagons. The hexagons transform gradually into tessellating men. Once the design moves from the village, it clearly lies on top of a grid of hexagons, as shown in Illustration 11.6. As you look at the grid, notice that the hats of the men, formed from two sides of a hexagon, remain constant as other details are gradually transformed. Notice, too, that Escher worked in

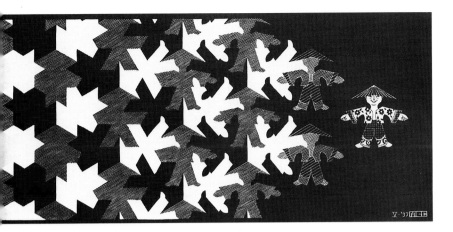

columns, just as we saw in the geometric designs in Illustrations 11.4 and 11.5. Thirteen rows and thirteen distinct motifs complete the transition, as detailed in Illustration 11.6.

Escher's Legacy

The jigsaw like puzzles of M. C. Escher, where shapes twist and turn, tessellating across a plane into new forms, have tantalized designers for decades. A master of the rules of symmetry and the formation of tessellations, Escher is an inspiration for today's artists in every surface design medium. Once I uncovered Escher's work and discovered the beauty of its rigorous design principles, I found exciting ways to apply it to my own work in quiltmaking and fabric design. Tessellations are a particularly rich alternative to traditional quilt forms.

My purpose in writing this book has been to help you understand how Escher achieved the representational images for which he is celebrated and how artisans before him used the same principles to create geometric designs that share the same characteristics. It is my hope that you will be able to apply the knowledge, techniques, and inspirations you find here to begin your own experiments. Escher was an extraordinary artist whose imagination knew no bounds and whose adherence to mathematical principles gave his work its mesmerizing quality. Escher opened the door for us to use tessellations in our own designs, making our road to discovery an easier one.

Appendix A

Patterns representing each of the 17 two-dimensional symmetries are shown on page 22. Below, each pattern is identified.

Author Notation	Standard Label	Cell	Tile
1. Six Rotation	p6		
2. Midpoint Rotation	p2		
3. Mirrored Pinwheel	p4g		
4. Mirror	pm		
5. Pinwheel	p4		
6. Staggered Mirror	cm		
7. Glide	pg		
8. Double Glide	pgg		
9. Kaleidoscope	p6m		
10. Double Mirror	pmm		
11. Staggered Double Mirror	cmm		
12. Traditional Block	p4m		
13. Three Rotation	p3		
14. Translation	p1		
15. Mirror and Three Rotations	p3m1		
16. Glided Staggered Mirror	pmg		
17. Three Rotations and a Mirror	p31m		

Appendix B

Patterns representing each of the 7 linear symmetries are shown on page 23. Below, each pattern is identified.

Author Notation	Standard Label	Cell	Tile
1. Translation	11		
2. Glide	1g		
3. Vertical Mirror	m1		
4. Horizontal Mirror	1m		
5. Double Mirror	mm		
6. Glided Mirror	mg		
7. Midpoint Rotation	12		

Appendix C

Symmetry Operation	Cell	Tile	Pattern
1. p31m			
2. p3m1			
3. p31m			
4. p3m1			
5. p3m1			
6. p3m1			

Answers to Exercise 5, page 135, *Altered Shapes Translated.* All four sides of shapes 1, 2, 4, and 5 can be altered by translation. All six sides of shapes of shapes 12 and 13 can be altered by translation. No other shapes on the page can be altered by translation.

Answers to Exercise 2, page 105, *Finding the Primary Cell*

Pattern	Primary Cell	Number of Cells in Tile	Symmetry
1. Tetra		4	Pinwheel (p4)
2. Geode		8	Traditional Block (p4m)
3. Discovery		4	Double Glide (pgg)
4. Lone Pine		2	Staggered Mirror (cm)
5. Arrowhead		4	Glided Staggered Mirror (pmg)
6. Desert Sun		4	Double Mirror (pmm)
7. Origami		3	Three Rotation (p3)
8. Spinning Sunflower		6	Six Rotation (p6)
9. Fractured Star		12	Kaleidoscope (p6m)
10. Triage		6	Mirror and Three Rotations (p3m1)
11. Spider Web		6	Three Rotations and a Mirror (p31m)
12. Angelica		4	Mirror (pm)
13. Lattice Work		16	Mirrored Pinwheel (p4g)
14. Infinity		2	Glide (pg)
15. Fantail		1	Translation (p1)
16. Strata		2	Midpoint Rotation (p2)
17. Paper Lantern		8	Staggered Double Mirror (cmm)

Answers to Exercise 6, page 139. All shapes on page 135 can be altered with a glide with the exception of 11, 14, and 15. All of the sides on shapes 1, 2, 3, 4, 5, 12, and 13 can be glided, but with 12 and 13, only four sides can be done at any one time. Two of the sides in triangles 7, 8, 9, and 10 can be altered with a glide, because those triangles have two sides that are equal in length.

Credits

All illustrations by Kandy Petersen.

Photographs courtesy the author: vii (top), xiv, 2, 11 (flower, cage, gazelles, ivy, window, fern, monkeys, columns), 13 (center and bottom), 14, 15, 38 (top right), 48 (bottom right), 71, 72, 86, 89, 90 (bottom center), 92 (bottom left), 94, 121 (top and bottom left), 153, 177, 208.

Photographs by Steve Tuttle: viii, x, xi, 8, 12, 13 (top), 30, 41, 44, 49, 52, 56, 58, 61, 64, 66, 73, 78, 79, 84, 93 (bottom right), 98, 122, 124, 133, 140, 147, 148, 150, 151, 152, 154, 155, 166, 174, 175, 176, 180, 193, 196, 200, 207, 209, 211, 212, 231, 233.

Art by M. C. Escher: *Symmetry Drawings E128*, 3 (top left), 35 (top); *E120/121*, 3 (top right), 220; *E24*, 3 (bottom left); *E25* (Reptiles), 3 (bottom right), 127; *E73* (Flying Fish), 134 (top); *E128* (Bird), 203; *E90* (Fish), 205; *E72* (Fish/Boat), 219; *E119*, 221; *E81*, 224; *E85*, 225.
Wall Mosaic in the Alhambra, 202.
Reptiles, 228.
Metamorphosis I, 236–37.
All M. C. Escher art copyright © 1998 Cordon Art B.V., Baarn, Holland. All rights reserved.

H. Armstrong Roberts: school of fish, copyright © Frink/Waterhouse/ H. Armstrong Roberts, 11; snow crystals, copyright © Sauer/Zefa/H. Armstrong Roberts, 11; butterfly, copyright © H. Armstrong Roberts, 11; windmill, copyright © R. Kord/H. Armstrong Roberts, 11; peacock, copyright © J. Moss/H. Armstrong Roberts, 11; migrating geese, copyright © A. McWhirter/H. Armstrong Roberts, 11.

Roger Foley: Governor's Palace garden and Wythe House, Williamsburg, Virginia, copyright © 1995 Roger Foley, 11.

U.S. Playing Card Company, Cincinnati: 37.

Textile Museum, Washington, D.C.: Iranian saddle blanket, no. 1961.39.5, gift of Arthur D. Jenkins, 38 (bottom).

Archive Photos: Abraham Lincoln courtesy Archive Photos, 120 (top); Edgar Allan Poe courtesy Archive Photos, 120 (center); Vivien Leigh courtesy American Stock/Archive Photos, 120 (bottom).

Auguste Racinet, from *L'Ornement polychrome*, published by Dover Publications, Inc.: 121 (bottom right), 182.